Cookbook
& Recipe Cards

Publications International, Ltd.

Special thanks to the Campbell's Kitchen and Jane M. Freiman, Group Manager.

Pictured on the front cover *(clockwise from top left)*: Toasted Corn & Sage Harvest Risotto *(page 84)*, Pan-Sautéed Chicken with Vegetables & Herbs *(page 77)*, Sensational Chicken Noodle Soup *(page 22)*, and Roast Pork with Green Apples & Golden Squash *(page 52)*.

Pictured on the back cover: Herb Roasted Turkey with Pan Gravy *(page 58)*.

ISBN-13: 978-1-4508-0908-5
ISBN-10: 1-4508-0908-1

Library of Congress Control Number: 2010931043

Manufactured in China.

8 7 6 5 4 3 2 1

Microwave Cooking: Microwave ovens vary in wattage. Use the cooking times as guidelines and check for doneness before adding more time.

Preparation/Cooking Times: Preparation times are based on the approximate amount of time required to assemble the recipe before cooking, baking, chilling or serving. These times include preparation steps such as measuring, chopping and mixing. The fact that some preparations and cooking can be done simultaneously is taken into account. Preparation of optional ingredients and serving suggestions is not included.

RECIPES TO **SHARE**

All cooks love to impress their guests with a delicious dish—and there's no better complement than being asked for a copy of the recipe. **Swanson®** *Cookbook & Recipe Cards* is the perfect resource for preparing your favorite dish, then sharing the recipe with your family and friends.

Forty-eight tasty recipes await you, each with step-by-step instructions and a mouthwatering photo of the final dish. And for each recipe, you'll also find a recipe card to tear out and share with others.

Why not impress your guests with a satisfying soup like Hearty Chicken Tortilla Soup? Or, give a comforting entrée, like Pork Chop Skillet Dinner, a try. Your next dinner party will be a hit with Rosemary Lamb Chops with Lemon Sauce. And, of course, your holiday will be complete with Layered Cranberry Walnut Stuffing.

You'll find recipes for every day and special days just waiting for you and your family and friends to enjoy.

CONTENTS

COOKBOOK

Hearty Chicken Tortilla Soup

Simply Special Seafood Chowder

Beef Bourguignonne

Beef Teriyaki

Ultra Creamy Mashed Potatoes

SWANSON

RECIPE CARDS

SATISFYING **SOUPS**

Butternut Squash & Baby Spinach in a Savory Broth

MAKES 8 SERVINGS ■ **PREP:** 20 minutes ■ **COOK:** 35 minutes

- 2 tablespoons butter
- 1 small onion, finely chopped (about ½ cup)
- 2 cloves garlic, minced
- 1 small butternut squash, peeled, seeded and diced (about 4½ cups)
- 2 large carrots, diced (about 1 cup)
- 6 cups Swanson® Chicken Broth (Regular, Natural Goodness® *or* Certified Organic)
- ¼ teaspoon ground cinnamon
- 1 bag (6 ounces) baby spinach leaves

1. Heat the butter in a 6-quart saucepot over medium-high heat. Add the onion and cook until it's tender. Add the garlic and cook for 30 seconds. Stir in the squash and carrots and cook for 5 minutes.

2. Stir in the broth and cinnamon and heat to a boil. Reduce the heat to low. Cover and cook for 10 minutes or until the vegetables are tender.

3. Stir in the spinach and cook until the spinach is wilted. Season to taste.

■ **KITCHEN TIP**

Cooking the spinach just until it wilts in Step 3 helps it to maintain its vibrant green color.

Blue Cheese Potato Soup with Olive Tapenade

MAKES 12 SERVINGS ■ **PREP:** 25 minutes ■ **COOK:** 40 minutes

- 2 tablespoons olive oil
- 2 medium onions, chopped (about 1 cup)
- 5 cloves garlic, minced
- 6 cups Swanson® Vegetable Broth (Regular *or* Certified Organic)
- 4 pounds red potatoes, peeled and diced
- 1 tablespoon balsamic vinegar
- ⅓ cup crumbled blue cheese
- ½ cup prepared olive tapenade

1. Heat the oil in a 6-quart saucepot over medium heat. Add the onions and garlic and cook until they're tender.

2. Stir the broth and potatoes in the saucepot and heat to a boil. Reduce the heat to low. Cover and cook for 30 minutes or until the potatoes are tender.

3. Pour ⅓ of the broth mixture into a blender or food processor. Cover and blend until smooth. Pour the mixture into a large bowl. Repeat twice more with the remaining broth mixture. Return all of the puréed mixture to the saucepot. Stir in the vinegar and cheese. Increase the heat to medium. Cook for 5 minutes or until the mixture is hot and bubbling. Season as desired.

4. Divide the soup mixture among **12** serving bowls. Top **each** with **2 teaspoons** tapenade.

Twice-Baked Potato Soup

MAKES 8 SERVINGS ■ **PREP:** 10 minutes ■ **COOK:** 45 minutes

- 6 large baking potatoes, scrubbed and pricked with a fork
- 2 tablespoons butter
- 1 small sweet onion, finely chopped (about ½ cup)
- 5 cups Swanson® Chicken Broth (Regular, Natural Goodness® *or* Certified Organic)
- ¼ cup light cream
- 1 tablespoon chopped fresh chives
  Potato Toppers

1. Heat the oven to 425°F. Arrange the potatoes on a rack and bake for 30 minutes or until tender. Place the potatoes in a bowl with a lid and let steam. Remove the skin and mash pulp.

2. Heat the butter in a 3-quart saucepan. Add the onion and cook until tender. Add the broth and **5 cups** of the potato pulp.

3. Place ⅓ of the broth mixture into an electric blender or food processor container. Cover and blend until smooth. Place in a medium bowl. Repeat the blending process with the remaining broth mixture. Return all of the puréed mixture into the saucepan. Stir in the cream and chives and cook for 5 minutes more. Season to taste.

4. Place ¼ **cup** of the remaining pulp mixture in **each** of **8** serving bowls. Divide the broth mixture among the bowls. Serve with one or more *Potato Toppers*.

Potato Toppers: Cooked crumbled bacon, shredded Cheddar cheese **and/ or** sour cream.

■ KITCHEN TIP

Microwave the potatoes on HIGH for 10 to 12 minutes or until fork-tender.

Slow-Simmered Chicken Rice Soup

MAKES 8 SERVINGS ■ **PREP:** 10 minutes ■ **COOK:** 7 hours 15 minutes

½ cup *uncooked* wild rice

½ cup *uncooked* regular long-grain white rice

1 tablespoon vegetable oil

5¼ cups Swanson® Chicken Broth (Regular, Natural Goodness® *or* Certified Organic)

2 teaspoons dried thyme leaves, crushed

¼ teaspoon crushed red pepper

2 stalks celery, coarsely chopped (about 1 cup)

1 medium onion, chopped (about ½ cup)

1 pound skinless, boneless chicken breasts, cut into cubes

Sour cream (optional)

Chopped green onions (optional)

1. Stir the wild rice, white rice and oil in a 3½-quart slow cooker. Cover and cook on HIGH for 15 minutes.

2. Add the broth, thyme, red pepper, celery, onion and chicken to the cooker. Turn the heat to LOW. Cover and cook for 7 to 8 hours* or until the chicken is cooked through.

3. Serve with the sour cream and green onions, if desired.

Or on HIGH for 4 to 5 hours.

■ **KITCHEN TIP**

*Speed preparation by substituting **3 cans** (4.5 ounces **each**) Swanson® Premium Chunk Chicken Breast, drained, for the raw chicken.*

Roasted Vegetable Soup with Garlic Herb Drizzle

MAKES 8 SERVINGS ■ **PREP:** 15 minutes ■ **BAKE:** 25 minutes ■ **COOK:** 30 minutes

- 1 **small bulb garlic**
- 7 **tablespoons olive oil**
- 1 **pound white potatoes, cut into cubes**
- 1 **small bulb fennel, cut into cubes**
- 2 **carrots, chopped (about 1 cup)**
- 1 **medium sweet onion, chopped (about 1 cup)**
- 6 **cups Swanson® Vegetable Broth (Regular *or* Certified Organic)**
- ¼ **cup finely chopped fresh basil *and/or* parsley leaves**

1. Heat the oven to 425°F. Cut ⅓ off the top of the garlic bulb and discard. Place remaining garlic on a piece of aluminum foil. Drizzle with **1 tablespoon** of the olive oil and wrap. Arrange the potatoes, fennel, carrots and onion in a 17×11-inch roasting pan. Pour **2 tablespoons** of the oil over the vegetables and toss to coat. Season to taste. Bake the vegetables and garlic for 25 minutes.

2. Place **1 cup** of the broth with the vegetable mixture into an electric blender or food processor container. Cover and blend until coarsely puréed. Pour the mixture into a 3-quart saucepan.

3. Add the remaining broth. Cook over high heat to a boil. Reduce the heat to low. Cook for 5 minutes.

4. Meanwhile, peel and smash the garlic in a small bowl. Add the basil and remaining oil.

5. Divide the soup among **8** serving bowls. Top **each** with **about 1 tablespoon** of the herbed oil mixture.

Thai Roasted Squash Soup

MAKES 6 SERVINGS ■ **PREP:** 35 minutes ■ **COOK:** 50 minutes

- 2 tablespoons vegetable oil
- 2 teaspoons curry powder
- 1 butternut squash, peeled, seeded and cut into 2-inch pieces (about 6 cups)
- 1 large sweet onion, cut into eighths
- 1 tablespoon chopped fresh ginger root
- 3 cups Swanson® Chicken Broth (Regular, Natural Goodness® *or* Certified Organic)
- 1 can (15 ounces) cream of coconut
- 3 tablespoons chopped fresh cilantro leaves

1. Heat the oven to 425°F. Stir the oil and curry in a large bowl. Add the squash and onions and toss to coat. Spread the vegetables onto a 17×11-inch roasting pan.

2. Bake for 25 minutes until the vegetables are golden brown, stirring occasionally.

3. Heat the vegetables, ginger root, broth and cream of coconut in a 4-quart saucepan over medium-high heat to a boil. Reduce the heat to low. Cook for 20 minutes or until the vegetables are tender.

4. Spoon ⅓ of the vegetable mixture into a blender or food processor. Cover and blend until smooth. Pour the mixture into a large bowl. Repeat the blending process twice more with the remaining vegetable mixture. Return all of the puréed mixture to the saucepan. Cook over medium heat until the mixture is hot. Season to taste. Divide the soup among **6** serving bowls. Sprinkle with the cilantro.

Hearty Chicken Tortilla Soup

MAKES 6 SERVINGS ■ **PREP:** 10 minutes ■ **COOK:** 30 minutes

Vegetable cooking spray

4　skinless, boneless chicken breasts, cut into 1-inch pieces (about 1 pound)

3½　cups Swanson® Chicken Broth (Regular, Natural Goodness® *or* Certified Organic)

1　teaspoon ground cumin

½　cup *uncooked* regular long-grain white rice

1　can (11 ounces) whole kernel corn with red and green peppers, drained

1　cup Pace® Picante Sauce

1　tablespoon chopped fresh cilantro leaves

2　tablespoons fresh lime juice

　Crisp Tortilla Strips

1. Spray a 6-quart saucepot with the cooking spray. Heat over medium-high heat for 1 minute. Add the chicken to the saucepot. Cook until it's browned, stirring often.

2. Stir the broth, cumin and rice in the saucepot. Heat to a boil. Reduce the heat to low. Cover and cook for 20 minutes.

3. Stir the corn, picante sauce, cilantro and lime juice in the saucepot. Cook until the rice is tender. Top **each** serving of soup with *Crisp Tortilla Strips*.

Crisp Tortilla Strips: Heat the oven to 425°F. Cut **4** corn tortillas into thin strips and place them on a baking sheet. Spray with the cooking spray. Bake for 10 minutes or until golden.

■ **KITCHEN TIP**

Use a pastry wheel when cutting the tortillas to create a special touch for the soup garnish.

Madeira Mushroom and Leek Soup

MAKES 6 SERVINGS ■ **PREP:** 10 minutes ■ **STAND:** 30 minutes
COOK: 1 hour 15 minutes

6	cups Swanson® Vegetable Broth (Regular *or* Certified Organic)
½	cup Madeira wine
1	ounce dried shiitake, morel *or* cépes mushrooms
4	tablespoons butter
3	leeks, white part only, coarsely chopped (about 2 cups)
2	tablespoons all-purpose flour
1	package (8 ounces) sliced white mushrooms (about 3 cups)
¼	teaspoon ground black pepper
	Additional chopped mushrooms *and* chopped leeks

1. Heat **1 cup** broth, wine and dried mushrooms in a 1-quart saucepan over high heat to a boil. Remove the saucepan from the heat. Let stand for 30 minutes. Do not drain.

2. Heat the butter in a 4-quart saucepan over low heat. Add the leeks and cook until they're tender-crisp. Stir in the flour. Cook and stir for 5 minutes.

3. Gradually stir in the remaining broth, fresh mushrooms, black pepper and the dried mushroom mixture. Heat to a boil. Reduce the heat to low and cook for 30 minutes or until the mushrooms are tender.

4. Place ⅓ of the mushroom mixture into a blender or food processor. Cover and blend until the mixture is smooth. Pour the mixture into a large bowl. Repeat twice more with the remaining mushroom mixture. Return all the puréed mixture to the saucepan. Cook over medium heat for 5 minutes or until the mixture is hot and bubbling.

5. Divide the soup among **6** serving bowls. Garnish with the additional mushrooms and leeks.

■ KITCHEN TIP

Madeira is a golden-colored wine that can be used for drinking as well as cooking. American-made Madeiras are often much more reasonably priced than the Portuguese originals.

Sensational Chicken Noodle Soup

MAKES 4 SERVINGS ■ **PREP:** 5 minutes ■ **COOK:** 25 minutes

4	cups Swanson® Chicken Broth (Regular, Natural Goodness® *or* Certified Organic)
	Generous dash ground black pepper
1	**medium carrot, sliced (about ½ cup)**
1	**stalk celery, sliced (about ½ cup)**
½	**cup *uncooked* extra wide egg noodles**
1	**cup shredded cooked chicken *or* turkey**

1. Heat the broth, black pepper, carrot and celery in a 2-quart saucepan over medium-high heat to a boil.

2. Stir the noodles and chicken into the saucepan. Reduce the heat to medium. Cook for 10 minutes or until the noodles are tender.

Asian Soup: Add **2** green onions cut into ½-inch pieces, **1 clove** garlic, minced, **1 teaspoon** ground ginger and **2 teaspoons** soy sauce. Substitute **uncooked** curly Asian noodles for egg noodles.

Mexican Soup: Add ½ **cup** Pace® Chunky Salsa, **1 clove** garlic, minced, **1 cup** rinsed and drained black beans and ½ **teaspoon** chili powder. Substitute **2** corn tortillas (4 or 6-inch) cut into thin strips for the noodles, adding them just before serving.

Italian Tortellini Soup: Add **1 can** (about 14.5 ounces) diced tomatoes, drained, **1 clove** garlic, minced, **1 teaspoon** dried Italian seasoning, crushed and **1 cup** spinach leaves. Substitute ½ **cup** frozen cheese tortellini for egg noodles. Serve with grated Parmesan cheese.

Roasted Squash Soup with Crispy Bacon

MAKES 6 SERVINGS ■ **PREP:** 15 minutes ■ **BAKE:** 25 minutes ■ **COOK:** 5 minutes

1   **small butternut squash (about 1½ pounds), diced (about 4 cups)**
2   **large onions, sliced (about 2 cups)**
3   **tablespoons olive oil**
3   **cups Swanson® Chicken Broth (Regular, Natural Goodness® *or* Certified Organic)**
½   **cup heavy cream**
¼   **cup real bacon bits**

1. Heat the oven to 425°F. Place the squash and onions in a 17×11-inch roasting pan. Add the oil and toss to coat. Bake for 25 minutes or until the squash is tender.

2. Place ½ of the squash mixture, **1½ cups** of the broth and ¼ **cup** of the cream in an electric blender or food processor container. Cover and blend until smooth. Pour the mixture into a medium bowl. Repeat the blending process with the remaining squash mixture, broth and cream. Season to taste. Return all of the puréed mixture to a 3-quart saucepan. Cook over medium heat for 5 minutes or until hot.

3. Divide the soup among **6** serving bowls. Top **each** serving of soup with **2 teaspoons** of the bacon.

■ **KITCHEN TIP**

Ready-cut butternut squash is sold in 20-ounce bags in the produce section, or you may also find it in the frozen foods section of your supermarket.

Asian Chicken Noodle Soup

MAKES 4 SERVINGS ■ **PREP:** 5 minutes ■ **COOK:** 20 minutes

3½   cups Swanson® Chicken Broth (Regular, Natural Goodness® *or* Certified Organic)
1   teaspoon soy sauce
1   teaspoon ground ginger
     Generous dash ground black pepper
1   medium carrot, diagonally sliced
1   stalk celery, diagonally sliced
½   red pepper, cut into 2-inch-long strips
2   green onions, diagonally sliced
1   clove garlic, minced
½   cup broken-up *uncooked* curly Asian noodles
1   cup shredded cooked chicken

1. Heat the broth, soy sauce, ginger, black pepper, carrot, celery, red pepper, green onions and garlic in a 2-quart saucepan over medium-high heat to a boil.

2. Stir the noodles and chicken in the saucepan. Reduce the heat to medium and cook for 10 minutes or until the noodles are done.

For an Interesting Twist: Use **1 cup** sliced bok choy for the celery and **2 ounces uncooked** cellophane noodles for the curly Asian noodles. Reduce the cook time to 5 minutes.

Roasted Chicken with Caramelized Onions Soup

MAKES 6 SERVINGS ■ **PREP:** 10 minutes ■ **COOK:** 30 minutes

2 teaspoons vegetable oil

2 medium onions, cut in half and thinly sliced (about 1 cup)

8 cups Swanson® Chicken Broth (Regular, Natural Goodness® *or* Certified Organic)

⅛ teaspoon ground black pepper

2 medium carrots, sliced (about 1 cup)

2 stalks celery, sliced (about 1 cup)

¾ cup *uncooked* trumpet-shaped pasta (campanelle)

2 cups roasted chicken, cut into strips

1. Heat the oil in a 10-inch skillet over medium-high heat. Add the onions and cook until they begin to brown, stirring occasionally. Reduce the heat to medium. Cook until the onions are tender and caramelized, stirring occasionally. Remove the skillet from the heat.

2. Heat the broth, black pepper, carrots and celery in a 4-quart saucepan over medium-high heat to a boil. Stir the pasta and chicken in the saucepan. Reduce the heat to medium. Cook for 10 minutes or until the pasta is tender. Stir in the onions and serve immediately.

KITCHEN TIP

*Cut the peeled onions in half lengthwise. Place the halves cut-side down on the cutting surface. Slice **each** onion half in parallel cuts up to, but not through, the root. Cut the root end off to free the slices.*

COMFORTING CHILIS AND CHOWDERS

Corn & Red Pepper Chowder

MAKES 6 SERVINGS ■ **PREP:** 20 minutes ■ **COOK:** 45 minutes

- 2 tablespoons vegetable oil
- 1 large sweet onion, diced (about 1 cup)
- ¼ cup all-purpose flour
- 2 cloves garlic, minced
- 6 cups Swanson® Chicken Broth (Regular, Natural Goodness® *or* Certified Organic)
- 2 medium Yukon gold potatoes, diced (about 2 cups)
- 2 cups fresh whole kernel corn *or* 1 package (about 10 ounces) frozen whole kernel corn
- 1 jar (about 7 ounces) roasted red peppers, drained and chopped
- ½ cup heavy cream (optional)
- ⅓ cup chopped fresh basil leaves

1. Heat the oil in a 4-quart saucepan over medium heat. Add the onion and cook until it's tender. Stir in the flour and garlic. Cook and stir for 1 minute.

2. Stir the broth and potatoes in the saucepan. Heat to a boil. Reduce the heat to low and cook for 20 minutes or until the potatoes are tender.

3. Stir the corn and red peppers in the saucepan. Cook for 10 minutes.

4. Add the cream, if desired, and ¼ **cup** of the basil. Season to taste. Divide the soup among **6** serving bowls. Sprinkle **each** serving of soup with the remaining basil.

Crab and Corn Chowder

MAKES 6 SERVINGS ■ **PREP:** 15 minutes ■ **COOK:** 35 minutes

4   slices bacon

1   large sweet onion, coarsely chopped (about 1 cup)

2   cloves garlic, minced

6   cups Swanson® Chicken Broth (Regular, Natural Goodness® *or* Certified Organic)

2   teaspoons seafood seasoning

6   to 8 red potatoes *or* fingerling potatoes, cut into 1-inch pieces (about 2 cups)

2   cups frozen whole kernel corn

1   container (8 ounces) refrigerated pasteurized lump crabmeat

½   cup heavy cream

1. Cook the bacon in a 4-quart saucepan over medium-high heat for 5 minutes or until it's crisp. Remove the bacon with a fork or kitchen tongs and drain on paper towels. Crumble the bacon and set aside. Pour off all but **2 tablespoons** drippings.

2. Reduce the heat to medium. Add the onion and garlic to the saucepan and cook until the onion is tender.

3. Stir the broth, seafood seasoning, potatoes and corn in the saucepan. Heat to a boil. Reduce the heat to low and cook for 15 minutes or until the potatoes are tender.

4. Stir in the crabmeat and cream and cook for 5 minutes or until the mixture is hot and bubbling. Divide the chowder among **6** serving bowls. Top **each** with **about 1 tablespoon** bacon.

■ **KITCHEN TIP**

If you can't find sweet onions, regular white **or** *yellow onions will work in this recipe.*

Simply Special Seafood Chowder

MAKES 6 SERVINGS ■ **PREP:** 10 minutes ■ **COOK:** 20 minutes

1 tablespoon olive oil *or* vegetable oil

1 medium bulb fennel, trimmed, halved and thinly sliced (about 2 cups)

1 medium onion, chopped (about ½ cup)

1 teaspoon dried thyme leaves, crushed

5 cups water

1¾ cups Swanson® Vegetable Broth (Regular *or* Certified Organic)

1 can (10¾ ounces) Campbell's® Condensed Tomato Soup

1 package (about 10 ounces) frozen whole baby carrots, thawed (about 1½ cups)

½ pound fresh *or* thawed frozen firm white fish fillet (cod, haddock *or* halibut), cut into 2-inch pieces

½ pound fresh large shrimp, peeled and deveined

¾ pound mussels (about 12), well scrubbed and beards removed

Freshly ground black pepper

1. Heat the oil in a 6-quart saucepot over medium heat. Add the fennel, onion and thyme and cook until they're tender. Stir the water, broth, soup and carrots in the saucepot and heat to a boil.

2. Add the fish. Cover and cook over medium heat for 2 minutes. Discard any open or cracked mussels. Add the shrimp and mussels. Cover and simmer for 3 minutes or until the fish flakes easily with a fork, the shrimp are pink and the mussels open. Discard any mussels that do not open. Sprinkle with black pepper.

Black Bean, Corn and Turkey Chili

MAKES 6 SERVINGS ■ **PREP:** 15 minutes ■ **COOK:** 40 minutes

1	tablespoon vegetable oil
1	pound ground turkey
1	large onion, chopped (about 1 cup)
2	tablespoons chili powder
1	teaspoon ground cumin
1	teaspoon dried oregano leaves, crushed
½	teaspoon ground black pepper
¼	teaspoon garlic powder *or* 2 cloves garlic, minced
1¾	cups Swanson® Chicken Stock
1	cup Pace® Picante Sauce
1	tablespoon sugar
1	can (about 15 ounces) black beans, rinsed and drained
1	can (about 16 ounces) whole kernel corn, drained

1. Heat the oil in a 4-quart saucepan over medium-high heat. Add the turkey, onion, chili powder, cumin, oregano, black pepper and garlic powder. Cook until the turkey is well browned, stirring often to separate meat.

2. Stir the stock, picante sauce, sugar, beans and corn in the saucepan and heat to a boil. Reduce the heat to low. Cover and cook for 30 minutes or until the mixture is hot and bubbling.

Poblano Corn Chowder with Chicken and Chorizo

MAKES 8 SERVINGS ■ **PREP:** 15 minutes ■ **COOK:** 8 hours

- **4** cups Swanson® Chicken Broth (Regular, Natural Goodness® *or* Certified Organic)
- **1** tablespoon sugar
- **2** cans (14.5 ounces *each*) cream-style corn
- **1** large potato, diced (about 2 cups)
- **2** large poblano chiles, seeded and diced (about 2 cups)
- **1** package (10 ounces) frozen whole kernel corn, thawed
- **1** pound skinless, boneless chicken (breasts *and/or* thighs), cut into cubes
- **½** pound chorizo sausage, diced
- **1** cup heavy cream
- **¼** cup chopped fresh cilantro

Place the broth, sugar, canned corn, potato, chiles, frozen corn, chicken and sausage in a 6-quart slow cooker. Cover and cook on LOW for 8 hours*. Stir in the cream and cilantro.

Or on HIGH for 4 hours.

KITCHEN TIP

*To enhance the flavor of the chowder, roast the chiles and corn before adding to the cooker. Place the chiles and thawed corn in a single layer in a roasting pan. Drizzle with **1 tablespoon** olive oil. Toss to coat. Bake at 375°F. for 30 minutes.*

Southwestern Chicken Chili

MAKES 6 SERVINGS ■ **PREP:** 15 minutes ■ **COOK:** 35 minutes

- 2 **tablespoons olive oil**
- 1 **cup chopped onion**
- ½ **cup chopped celery**
- ½ **cup chopped red pepper**
- 3 **tablespoons all-purpose flour**
- 1 **tablespoon ground cumin**
- 2 **cups Swanson® Chicken Stock**
- 2 **cans (15 ounces *each*) great Northern beans**
- 1 **jar (16 ounces) Pace® Picante Sauce**
- 2 **cups chopped cooked chicken**
  Shredded Pepper Jack cheese
  Cubed avocado

1. Heat the oil in a 4-quart saucepot over medium heat. Add the onion, celery and pepper and cook until they're tender. Stir in the flour and cumin and cook for 2 minutes. Stir the stock in the saucepot. Cook and stir until the mixture boils.

2. Stir the beans, picante sauce and chicken in the saucepot. Heat to a boil. Reduce the heat to low. Cook for 20 minutes.

3. Garnish with the cheese and avocado.

MEMORABLE
MAIN DISHES

Citrus Balsamic Salmon

MAKES 8 SERVINGS ■ **PREP:** 10 minutes ■ **BAKE:** 15 minutes
COOK: 5 minutes

- 8 salmon fillets, ¾-inch thick
   Ground black pepper
- 3 tablespoons olive oil
- 1¾ cups Swanson® Chicken Stock
- 3 tablespoons balsamic vinegar
- 1½ tablespoons cornstarch
- 1 tablespoon orange juice
- 1 tablespoon packed brown sugar
- 1 teaspoon grated orange zest
   Orange slices

1. Season the salmon with the black pepper. Place the salmon into a 2-quart shallow baking dish. Drizzle with the olive oil. Bake at 350°F. for 15 minutes or until the salmon flakes easily when tested with a fork.

2. Heat the stock, vinegar, cornstarch, orange juice, brown sugar and orange zest in a 2-quart saucepan over medium-high heat to a boil. Cook and stir until the mixture boils and thickens.

3. Serve the salmon with the citrus sauce. Garnish with the orange slices.

KITCHEN TIP

Salmon and sauce may be refrigerated separately and served chilled.

Savory Orange Chicken with Sage

MAKES 4 SERVINGS ■ **PREP:** 10 minutes ■ **COOK:** 20 minutes

- **4** skinless, boneless chicken breasts halves (about 1 pound)
- **½** cup all-purpose flour
- **1** tablespoon vegetable oil
- **1** tablespoon butter
- **1¾** cups Swanson® Chicken Stock
- **⅓** cup orange juice
- **¼** cup Chablis *or* other dry white wine
- **1** tablespoon grated orange zest
- **1** tablespoon chopped fresh sage leaves *or* 1 teaspoon ground sage
- **¼** teaspoon ground black pepper
- **2** cups chopped shiitake mushrooms (about 3½ ounces)

    Hot cooked rice

1. Coat the chicken with the flour.

2. Heat the oil and butter in a 12-inch skillet over medium-high heat. Add the chicken and cook for 10 minutes or until it's well browned on both sides. Remove the chicken from the skillet.

3. Stir the stock, juice, wine, orange zest, sage and black pepper in the skillet and heat to a boil. Stir in the mushrooms. Return the chicken to the skillet. Reduce the heat to low. Cook for 5 minutes or until the chicken is cooked through and liquid is reduced by one-fourth. Serve with the rice.

Almond-Crusted Salmon with Thyme & Lemon Butter Sauce

MAKES 8 SERVINGS ■ **PREP:** 15 minutes ■ **BAKE:** 15 minutes

- ¼ **cup plain dry bread crumbs**
- ¼ **cup blanched almonds**
- 1 **clove garlic**
- 2 **tablespoons olive oil**
- 8 **salmon fillets (about 3 pounds)**
- 1 **tablespoon cornstarch**
- 1½ **cups Swanson® Chicken Stock**
- 2 **tablespoons lemon juice**
- 1 **teaspoon chopped fresh thyme leaves** *or* ¼ **teaspoon dried thyme leaves, crushed**
- 3 **tablespoons butter**
- ¼ **cup chopped shallot** *or* **onion**

1. Place the bread crumbs, almonds and garlic into a food processor or blender. Cover and process until the mixture is finely ground. Gradually pour in the olive oil while the food processor is running and process until the mixture is moist.

2. Place the salmon into a roasting pan. Top the salmon with the bread crumb mixture and press to adhere.

3. Bake at 400°F. for 15 minutes or until the salmon flakes easily when tested with a fork and the bread crumb mixture is golden. Remove the salmon from the oven and keep warm.

4. Stir the cornstarch, stock, lemon juice and thyme in a medium bowl until the mixture is smooth.

5. Heat **2 tablespoons** butter in a 1-quart saucepan over medium heat. Add the shallots and cook until they're tender. Stir in the cornstarch mixture and heat to a boil. Cook and stir until the sauce boils and thickens. Add the remaining butter and cook and stir until it's melted. Serve the salmon with the sauce.

Holiday Brisket with Savory Onion Jus

MAKES 8 SERVINGS ■ **PREP:** 15 minutes ■ **COOK:** 3 hours 15 minutes
STAND: 10 minutes

- 2 tablespoons olive *or* vegetable oil
- 6 medium onions, cut into quarters (about 6 cups)
- 1 medium butternut squash (about 3 pounds), peeled, seeded and cut into 1½-inch cubes (about 6 cups)
  3-pound boneless beef brisket
- 1¾ cups Swanson® Beef Stock
- ½ cup orange juice
- ½ cup dry red wine
- ½ cup packed brown sugar
- 1 can (about 28 ounces) whole peeled tomatoes

1. Heat the oil in an 8-quart saucepot over medium-high heat. Add the onions and squash and cook over medium heat until they're tender-crisp. Remove the vegetables from the saucepot.

2. Season the beef as desired. Increase the heat to medium-high. Add the beef to the saucepot and cook until it's well browned on both sides. Remove the beef from the saucepot. Pour off any fat.

3. Add the stock, orange juice, wine, brown sugar and tomatoes to the saucepot and heat to a boil. Reduce the heat to low. Return the beef to the saucepot. Cover and cook for 2 hours.

4. Return the vegetables to the saucepot. Cover and cook for 1 hour or until the beef is fork-tender.

5. Remove the beef to a cutting board. Let stand for 10 minutes. Serve the beef with the vegetables and sauce.

Rosemary Lamb Chops with Lemon Sauce

MAKES 3 SERVINGS ▪ **PREP:** 5 minutes ▪ **COOK:** 15 minutes

- 6 **lamb chops (about ¾-inch thick)**
- 1 **teaspoon dried rosemary leaves, crushed**
- 1 **cup Swanson® Chicken Stock**
- 2 **teaspoons cornstarch**
- 1 **teaspoon lemon zest**
- 3 **tablespoons lemon juice**
- 3 **teaspoons Dijon-style mustard**

1. Heat the broiler. Season the lamb with the rosemary. Place the lamb on a broiler pan.

2. Broil for 10 minutes (for medium-rare) or to desired doneness, turning the lamb over once halfway through broiling.

3. Stir the stock and cornstarch in a 1-quart saucepan until the mixture is smooth. Stir in the lemon zest, lemon juice and mustard. Cook and stir over medium heat until the mixture boils and thickens. Serve the stock mixture with the lamb.

KITCHEN TIP

The lamb chops can also be grilled. Lightly oil the grill rack and heat the grill to medium. Grill the lamb for 10 minutes (for medium-rare) or to desired doneness, turning the lamb over once halfway through grilling. Serve with the stock mixture.

Savory Chicken Thighs with Figs

MAKES 6 SERVINGS ■ **PREP:** 10 minutes ■ **COOK:** 30 minutes

- 1½ **pounds boneless chicken thighs**
- 2 **tablespoons all-purpose flour**
- 1 **tablespoon olive oil**
- 1 **medium onion, chopped (about ½ cup)**
- 3 **cloves garlic, minced**
- 1 **cup Swanson® Chicken Stock**
- 2 **tablespoons balsamic vinegar**
- 1 **teaspoon dried thyme leaves, crushed**
- ¼ **teaspoon ground black pepper**
- 6 **ounces dried figs, stems removed and cut in half**
   Hot cooked rice

1. Coat the chicken with the flour.

2. Heat the oil in a 10-inch skillet over medium-high heat. Add the chicken in 2 batches and cook until it's well browned on both sides.

3. Add the onion and garlic to the skillet and cook until the onion is tender. Stir the stock, vinegar, thyme, black pepper and figs in the skillet and heat to a boil. Reduce the heat to low. Cover and cook for 10 minutes or until the chicken is cooked through. Serve with the rice.

KITCHEN TIP

Chicken thighs are an inexpensive ingredient that can taste rich and decadent. The balsamic vinegar and figs in this recipe perfectly balance the richness of the chicken.

Spiral Ham with Mango Salsa

MAKES 24 SERVINGS ■ **PREP:** 30 minutes ■ **BAKE:** 2 hours

- 1 **tablespoon butter**
- 1 **large onion, chopped (about 1 cup)**
- 1½ **cups Swanson® Chicken Stock**
- 1 **can (12 ounces) mango juice *or* nectar**
- 1 **package (4 ounces) dried mango, coarsely chopped**
- ⅓ **cup packed brown sugar**
- 4 **medium green onions, chopped (about ½ cup)**

  9-pound fully-cooked bone-in *or* 6-pound fully-cooked boneless spiral cut ham

1. Heat the butter in a 2-quart saucepan over medium-high heat. Add the onion and cook until it's tender. Stir in the stock, mango juice, dried mango and brown sugar and heat to a boil. Reduce the heat to low. Cook and stir for 10 minutes or until the mixture boils and thickens. Remove the saucepan from the heat and let the mixture cool slightly.

2. Place a strainer over a medium bowl. Pour the stock mixture through the strainer. Reserve the stock mixture for the glaze. Place the strained mango mixture into a small bowl. Stir in the green onions. Cover the bowl and refrigerate until serving time.

3. Place the ham in a 17×11-inch roasting pan and cover loosely with foil. Bake at 325°F. for 1½ hours. Remove the foil. Spoon the reserved stock mixture over the ham. Bake for 30 minutes more or until the internal temperature of the ham reaches 140°F., basting the ham frequently with the pan drippings. Serve the ham with the mango salsa.

KITCHEN TIP

Substitute chopped fresh cilantro leaves for the green onions.

Roast Pork with Green Apples & Golden Squash

MAKES 8 SERVINGS ■ **PREP:** 20 minutes ■ **COOK:** 45 minutes

	Vegetable cooking spray
2	(¾ pound *each*) whole pork tenderloins
1	teaspoon olive oil
¼	teaspoon coarsely ground black pepper
3	large Granny Smith apples, cored and thickly sliced
1	butternut squash (about 1½ pounds), peeled, seeded and cut into cubes
2	tablespoons packed brown sugar
½	teaspoon ground cinnamon
1	medium onion, chopped (about ½ cup)
1¾	cups Swanson® Chicken Stock
2	teaspoons all-purpose flour

1. Heat the oven to 425°F. Spray a roasting pan with the cooking spray.

2. Brush the pork with the oil and season with the black pepper. Place the pork in the pan. Stir the apples, squash, brown sugar, cinnamon, onion and ½ **cup** stock in a large bowl. Add the apple mixture to the pan.

3. Roast for 25 minutes or until the pork is cooked through, stirring the apple mixture once during roasting. Remove the pork from the pan and keep it warm. Roast the apple mixture for 15 minutes or until it's browned. Remove the apple mixture from the pan.

4. Stir the remaining stock and flour in a small bowl until the mixture is smooth. Stir the stock mixture in the pan. Cook and stir over medium-high heat until the mixture boils and thickens, scraping up the browned bits from the bottom of the pan. Serve the stock mixture with the pork and apple mixture.

Beef Bourguignonne

MAKES 4 SERVINGS ■ **PREP:** 10 minutes ■ **COOK:** 30 minutes

1	beef sirloin steak *or* top round steak (about 1 pound), cut into 1-inch pieces
¼	cup all-purpose flour
1	tablespoon olive oil
1	medium onion, chopped (about ½ cup)
2	cloves garlic, minced
⅛	teaspoon dried parsley flakes
¼	teaspoon ground black pepper
2	cups sliced mushrooms (about 6 ounces)
1	teaspoon dried thyme leaves, crushed
2	cups fresh *or* frozen whole baby carrots
1¾	cups Swanson® Beef Stock
½	cup Burgundy *or* other dry red wine
	Hot cooked orzo pasta

1. Coat the beef with the flour.

2. Heat the oil in a 10-inch skillet over medium-high heat. Add the beef and cook until it's well browned, stirring often. Add the onion, garlic, parsley, black pepper, mushrooms and thyme and cook until the mushrooms are tender.

3. Stir the carrots, stock and wine in the skillet and heat to a boil. Reduce the heat to low. Cover and cook for 20 minutes or until the beef is cooked through. Serve the beef mixture over the orzo.

Braised Beef with Shallots and Mushrooms

MAKES 4 SERVINGS ■ **PREP:** 20 minutes ■ **COOK:** 2 hours 35 minutes

- 1 **beef chuck pot roast, cut into serving-sized pieces (about 1½ pounds)**
- ¼ **cup all-purpose flour**
- 3 **tablespoons butter**
- ½ **pound small shallots, peeled**
- 1 **cup Swanson® Beef Stock**
- 2 **medium tomatoes, chopped (about 2 cups)**
- 3 **tablespoons balsamic vinegar**
- 1 **tablespoon packed brown sugar**
- 2 **large carrots, cut into 2-inch pieces (about 1 cup)**
- 2 **cups mushrooms, cut into quarters (about 5 ounces)**
- ¼ **cup chopped fresh parsley**
- 2 **tablespoons grated lemon zest**

1. Coat the beef with the flour. Heat the butter in a 12-inch skillet over medium-high heat. Add the beef and cook until it's well browned on all sides. Remove the beef from the skillet. Pour off any fat.

2. Add the shallots to the skillet. Cook for 10 minutes or until they're tender. Stir in the stock, tomatoes, vinegar and brown sugar and heat to a boil. Return the beef to the skillet. Reduce the heat to low. Cover and cook for 1½ hours.

3. Add the carrots and mushrooms to the skillet and cook for 30 minutes or until the beef is fork-tender and the vegetables are tender. Remove the beef and vegetables from the skillet and keep warm.

4. Increase the heat to high. Cook for 10 minutes or until the stock mixture is thickened. Return the beef and vegetables to the skillet. Season as desired. Sprinkle with the parsley and lemon zest.

Pork Chops with Cranberry Balsamic Sauce

MAKES 4 SERVINGS ■ **PREP:** 5 minutes ■ **COOK:** 30 minutes

- 4 **boneless pork chops, 1-inch thick**
  Lemon pepper seasoning
- 2 **tablespoons butter**
- 2 **cloves garlic, thinly sliced**
- 1¾ **cups Swanson® Chicken Stock**
- ¼ **cup balsamic vinegar**
- ½ **cup dried cranberries *or* dried cherries**

1. Season the pork with the lemon pepper. Cook the pork in a 10-inch nonstick skillet over medium heat for 20 minutes or until it's well browned on both sides and cooked through. Remove the pork from the skillet and keep warm.

2. Heat **1 tablespoon** butter in the skillet. Add the garlic and cook until it's tender. Stir the stock, vinegar and cranberries in the skillet and heat to a boil. Cook for 10 minutes or until the sauce is slightly thickened.

3. Stir in the remaining butter. Serve the pork with the sauce.

Herb Roasted Turkey with Pan Gravy

MAKES 12 SERVINGS ■ **PREP:** 15 minutes ■ **COOK:** 4 hours 20 minutes
STAND: 10 minutes

1¾ **cups Swanson® Chicken Stock**

3 **tablespoons lemon juice**

1 **teaspoon dried basil leaves, crushed**

1 **teaspoon dried thyme leaves, crushed**

⅛ **teaspoon ground black pepper**

1 **(12- to 14-pound) turkey**

¼ **cup all-purpose flour**

1. Stir the stock, lemon juice, basil, thyme and black pepper in a small bowl.

2. Roast the turkey according to the package directions, basting occasionally with the stock mixture during cooking. Let the turkey stand for 10 minutes before slicing.

3. Remove the turkey from the roasting pan. Spoon off any fat.

4. Stir the remaining stock mixture and flour in a small bowl until the mixture is smooth. Add the stock mixture to the roasting pan. Cook and stir over medium heat until the mixture boils and thickens. Serve the turkey with the gravy.

ONE DISH
PERFECTION

Sausage and Bean Ragoût

MAKES 6 SERVINGS ■ **PREP:** 15 minutes ■ **COOK:** 40 minutes

- 2 tablespoons olive oil
- 1 pound ground beef
- 1 pound hot Italian pork sausage, casing removed
- 1 large onion, chopped (about 1 cup)
- 4 cloves garlic, minced
- 3½ cups Swanson® Chicken Stock
- ¼ cup chopped fresh basil leaves
- 2 cans (14.5 ounces *each*) Italian-style diced tomatoes
- 1 can (about 15 ounces) white kidney beans (cannellini), rinsed and drained
- ½ cup *uncooked* elbow pasta
- 1 bag (6 ounces) fresh baby spinach leaves
- ⅓ cup grated Romano cheese

1. Heat the oil in a 6-quart saucepot over medium-high heat. Add the beef, sausage and onion and cook until the beef and sausage are well browned, stirring often to separate meat. Pour off any fat. Add the garlic and cook and stir for 30 seconds.

2. Stir the stock, basil, tomatoes and beans in the saucepot and heat to a boil. Reduce the heat to low. Cover and cook for 10 minutes, stirring occasionally. Add the pasta and cook until it's tender.

3. Stir in the spinach and cook until the spinach is wilted. Remove the saucepot from the heat and stir in the cheese. Serve with additional cheese, if desired.

■ KITCHEN TIP

This recipe calls for cooking the pasta until it's tender. However, if you like your pasta a little al dente, that will work as well.

Cavatelli with Sausage & Broccoli

MAKES 6 SERVINGS ■ **PREP:** 10 minutes ■ **COOK:** 30 minutes

1   package (1 pound) *uncooked* frozen narrow shell-shaped (cavatelli) pasta (about 3 cups)

1   tablespoon olive oil

1   pound sweet Italian pork sausage, casing removed

1   tablespoon butter

2   cloves garlic, minced

1   bag (about 16 ounces) frozen broccoli flowerets, thawed

2   cups Swanson® Chicken Stock

2   tablespoons grated Romano cheese

     Crushed red pepper flakes

1. Cook the pasta according to the package directions in a 6-quart saucepot. Drain the pasta well in a colander. Return the pasta to the saucepot.

2. Heat the oil in a 10-inch skillet over medium-high heat. Add the sausage and cook until it's well browned, stirring often to separate meat. Remove the sausage from the skillet. Pour off any fat.

3. Add the butter and garlic to the skillet. Reduce the heat to medium. Cook for 2 minutes or until the garlic is golden.

4. Add the broccoli to the skillet and cook for 5 minutes or until it's tender-crisp, stirring often. Stir in the stock and heat to a boil.

5. Add the broccoli mixture, sausage and cheese to the saucepot. Cook over medium heat for 10 minutes or until the stock mixture is thickened, stirring occasionally. Serve with the red pepper and additional cheese, if desired.

Easy One-Pot Spaghetti & Clams

MAKES 8 SERVINGS ■ **PREP:** 5 minutes ■ **COOK:** 20 minutes

3	tablespoons olive oil
3	cloves garlic, minced
¼	teaspoon crushed red pepper flakes
8	cups Swanson® Chicken Stock
1	can (6.5 ounces) chopped clams, undrained
1	package (1 pound) *uncooked* thin spaghetti
1	can (10 ounces) whole baby clams, undrained
16	littleneck clams, scrubbed
⅓	cup chopped fresh parsley

1. Heat the oil in a 4-quart saucepan over medium heat. Add the garlic and red pepper. Cook for 1 minute. Add the stock and chopped clams. Heat to a boil.

2. Add the spaghetti. Cook for about 9 minutes or until the stock is absorbed. Add the canned and fresh clams. Cook for 2 minutes or until the fresh clams open. Toss with the parsley.

■ **KITCHEN TIP**

If using fresh clams, the shells should be tightly closed. If the shells are open, tap them slightly and if they don't close shut, then the clam is no longer alive and should be discarded. Also, after cooking discard any clams that do not open.

Chicken Cacciatore & Pasta

MAKES 4 SERVINGS ■ **PREP:** 10 minutes ■ **COOK:** 30 minutes

1	tablespoon vegetable oil
4	skinless, boneless chicken breast halves (about 1 pound)
1¾	cups Swanson® Chicken Stock
1	teaspoon dried oregano leaves, crushed
1	teaspoon garlic powder
1	can (14.5 ounces) diced tomatoes
1	small green pepper, cut into 2-inch-long strips (about 1 cup)
1	medium onion, cut into wedges
¼	teaspoon ground black pepper
2½	cups *uncooked* medium shell-shaped pasta

1. Heat the oil in a 10-inch skillet over medium-high heat. Add the chicken and cook for 10 minutes or until it's well browned on both sides.

2. Stir the stock, oregano, garlic powder, tomatoes, green pepper, onion and black pepper in the skillet and heat to a boil. Stir in the pasta. Reduce the heat to low. Cover and cook for 15 minutes or until the pasta is tender.

Hearty Beef Stew

MAKES 4 SERVINGS ■ **PREP:** 15 minutes ■ **COOK:** 2 hours 15 minutes

1	pound beef for stew, cut into 1-inch pieces
3	tablespoons all-purpose flour
2	tablespoons olive oil
2	cloves garlic, minced
1¾	cups Swanson® Beef Stock
2	medium onions, cut into quarters
1	bay leaf
½	teaspoon dried thyme leaves, crushed
¼	teaspoon ground black pepper
2	cups whole baby carrots
2	medium potatoes, cut into 2-inch pieces
¼	cup water

1. Season the beef as desired. Coat with **1 tablespoon** flour. Heat the oil in a 6-quart saucepot over medium-high heat. Add the beef and cook until it's well browned, stirring often. Add the garlic to the saucepot and cook and stir for 1 minute.

2. Stir the stock, onions, bay leaf, thyme and black pepper in the saucepot and heat to a boil. Reduce the heat to low. Cover and cook for 1½ hours.

3. Add the carrots and potatoes to the saucepot. Cover and cook for 30 minutes or until the beef is fork-tender and the vegetables are tender. Remove and discard the bay leaf.

4. Stir the remaining flour and water in a small bowl until the mixture is smooth. Stir the flour mixture in the saucepot. Increase the heat to medium. Cook and stir until the mixture boils and thickens.

Greek-Style Beef Stew

MAKES 6 SERVINGS ■ **PREP:** 10 minutes ■ **COOK:** 8 hours

1	boneless beef bottom round roast *or* chuck pot roast (about 2 pounds), cut into 1-inch pieces
1	bag (16 ounces) frozen whole small white onions
1	bag (16 ounces) fresh *or* frozen whole baby carrots
2	tablespoons all-purpose flour
1¾	cups Swanson® Beef Stock
1	can (5.5 ounces) V8® 100% Vegetable Juice
1	tablespoon packed brown sugar
	Bouquet Garni
	Hot buttered noodles

1. Place the beef, onions and carrots into a 4-quart slow cooker. Sprinkle with the flour and toss to coat.

2. Stir the stock, vegetable juice and brown sugar in a medium bowl until the mixture is smooth. Pour the stock mixture over the beef and vegetables. Submerge the *Bouquet Garni* into the stock mixture.

3. Cover and cook on LOW for 8 to 9 hours* or until the beef is fork-tender. Remove the *Bouquet Garni*. Serve the beef mixture over the noodles.

Or on HIGH for 4 to 5 hours.

Bouquet Garni: Lay a 4-inch square of cheesecloth flat on the counter. Place ½ **teaspoon** whole cloves, **1** cinnamon stick and **1** bay leaf in the center of the cloth. Bring the corners of the cloth together and tie with kitchen string into a bundle.

Pork Chop Skillet Dinner

MAKES 4 SERVINGS ■ **PREP:** 10 minutes ■ **COOK:** 40 minutes

1	tablespoon olive oil
4	bone-in pork chops, ¾-inch thick *each*
1	medium onion, chopped (about ½ cup)
1	cup *uncooked* regular long-grain white rice
1¼	cups Swanson® Chicken Stock
1	cup orange juice
3	tablespoons chopped fresh parsley
¼	teaspoon ground black pepper
4	orange slices

1. Heat the oil in a 12-inch skillet over medium-high heat. Add the pork and cook until it's well browned on both sides.

2. Add the onion and rice to the skillet. Cook until the rice is lightly browned.

3. Stir in the stock, orange juice, **2 tablespoons** parsley and black pepper and heat to a boil. Reduce the heat to low. Cover and cook for 20 minutes or until the pork is cooked through and the rice is tender. Top with the orange slices and sprinkle with the remaining parsley.

Herb-Simmered Beef Stew

MAKES 6 SERVINGS ■ **PREP:** 15 minutes ■ **COOK:** 1 hour 30 minutes

- 2 **pounds beef for stew, cut into 1-inch cubes**
  Ground black pepper
- 2 **tablespoons all-purpose flour**
- 2 **tablespoons olive oil**
- 3 **cups thickly-sliced mushrooms (about 8 ounces)**
- 3 **cloves garlic, minced**
- ½ **teaspoon dried marjoram leaves, crushed *or* 1½ teaspoons fresh marjoram leaves**
- ½ **teaspoon dried thyme leaves, crushed *or* 1½ teaspoons fresh thyme leaves**
- ½ **teaspoon dried rosemary leaves, crushed *or* 1½ teaspoons fresh rosemary leaves**
- 1 **bay leaf**
- 1¾ **cups Swanson® Beef Stock**
- 3 **cups fresh *or* frozen whole baby carrots**
- 12 **whole small red potatoes**

1. Season the beef with the black pepper. Coat the beef with the flour.

2. Heat the oil in a 6-quart saucepot over medium-high heat. Add the beef in 2 batches and cook until it's well browned, stirring often. Pour off any fat.

3. Add the mushrooms, garlic, herbs and bay leaf to the saucepot and cook until the mushrooms are tender. Stir in the stock and heat to a boil. Reduce the heat to low. Cover and cook for 45 minutes.

4. Increase the heat to medium-high. Stir in the carrots and potatoes and heat to a boil. Reduce the heat to low. Cover and cook for 30 minutes or until the beef is fork-tender. Remove and discard the bay leaf.

■■ **KITCHEN TIP**

For visual interest, you can peel a strip around the centers of the potatoes before cooking.

Beef Teriyaki

MAKES 4 SERVINGS ■ **PREP:** 10 minutes ■ **COOK:** 15 minutes

2	**tablespoons cornstarch**
1¾	**cups Swanson® Beef Stock**
2	**tablespoons soy sauce**
1	**tablespoon packed brown sugar**
½	**teaspoon garlic powder**
1	**boneless beef sirloin steak**
4	**cups fresh *or* frozen broccoli flowerets**
	Hot cooked rice

1. Stir the cornstarch, stock, soy sauce, brown sugar and garlic powder in a small bowl until the mixture is smooth.

2. Stir-fry the beef in a 10-inch nonstick skillet over medium-high heat until it's well browned, stirring often. Pour off any fat.

3. Add the broccoli to the skillet and cook for 1 minute. Stir in the cornstarch mixture. Cook and stir until the mixture boils and thickens. Serve the beef mixture over the rice.

KITCHEN TIP

To make slicing easier, freeze the beef for 1 hour before slicing.

Pan-Sautéed Chicken with Vegetables & Herbs

MAKES 4 SERVINGS ■ **PREP:** 20 minutes ■ **COOK:** 1 hour

⅛ teaspoon ground black pepper

⅛ teaspoon paprika

2 tablespoons all-purpose flour

4 bone-in chicken breast halves (about 2 pounds)

2 tablespoons olive oil

2 small red onions, cut into quarters

1 pound new potatoes, cut into quarters

8 ounces fresh whole baby carrots (about 16), green tops trimmed to 1-inch-long

1½ cups Swanson® Chicken Stock

3 tablespoons lemon juice

1 tablespoon chopped fresh oregano leaves

Chopped fresh thyme leaves (optional)

1. Heat the oven to 350°F. Stir the black pepper, paprika and flour on a plate. Coat the chicken with the flour mixture.

2. Heat the oil in a 12-inch oven-safe skillet over medium-high heat. Add the chicken and cook until it's well browned on all sides. Remove the chicken from the skillet.

3. Add the onions and potatoes to the skillet and cook for 5 minutes. Add the carrots, stock, lemon juice and oregano and heat to a boil. Return the chicken to the skillet. Cover the skillet.

4. Bake for 20 minutes. Uncover the skillet and bake for 15 minutes or until the chicken is cooked through and the vegetables are tender. Sprinkle with the thyme, if desired.

SUPER **SIDES**

Harvest Fruit Stuffing

MAKES 8 SERVINGS ■ **PREP:** 10 minutes ■ **COOK:** 10 minutes
BAKE: 20 minutes

1¾   **cups Swanson® Chicken Broth (Regular, Natural Goodness® *or* Certified Organic)**

¼   **cup apple juice**

1   **cup cut-up mixed dried fruit**

1   **stalk celery, sliced (about ½ cup)**

1   **medium onion, chopped (about ½ cup)**

5   **cups Pepperidge Farm® Herb Seasoned Stuffing**

1. Heat the oven to 350°F.

2. Stir the broth, apple juice, dried fruit, celery and onion in a 3-quart saucepan. Heat to a boil over medium-high heat. Reduce the heat to low. Cover and cook for 5 minutes or until the vegetables are tender. Remove the saucepan from the heat. Add the stuffing and stir lightly to coat.

3. Spoon the stuffing into 1½-quart casserole. Bake for 20 minutes or until it's hot.

Roasted Asparagus with Lemon & Goat Cheese

MAKES 6 SERVINGS ■ **PREP:** 10 minutes ■ **COOK:** 20 minutes

Vegetable cooking spray

2 **pounds asparagus, trimmed**

1 **tablespoon olive oil**

Freshly ground black pepper

½ **cup Swanson® Vegetable Broth**

3 **ounces soft goat cheese, crumbled**

1 **tablespoon lemon juice**

1 **teaspoon grated lemon peel**

1. Heat the oven to 425°F. Spray a 17×11-inch roasting pan or shallow baking sheet with the cooking spray.

2. Stir the asparagus and oil in the pan. Season with the black pepper. Pour in the broth.

3. Roast the asparagus for 20 minutes or until it's tender, stirring once during cooking. Top with the cheese, lemon juice and lemon peel.

Pumpkin Apple Mash

MAKES 4 SERVINGS ■ **PREP:** 10 minutes ■ **COOK:** 20 minutes

2	tablespoons butter
1	small onion, chopped (about ¼ cup)
¾	cup Swanson® Chicken Broth (Regular, Natural Goodness® *or* Certified Organic)
1	tablespoon packed brown sugar
¼	teaspoon dried thyme leaves, crushed
⅛	teaspoon ground black pepper
1	pumpkin *or* calabaza squash (about 2½ pounds), peeled, seeded and cut into 1-inch pieces (about 5 to 6 cups)
2	medium McIntosh apples, peeled, cored and cut into 1-inch pieces

1. Heat the butter in a 4-quart saucepan over medium-high heat. Add the onion and cook until the onion is tender-crisp.

2. Stir the broth, brown sugar, thyme, black pepper and pumpkin in the saucepan and heat to a boil. Reduce the heat to low. Cover and cook for 10 minutes or until the pumpkin is tender.

3. Stir the apples in the saucepan. Cook for 5 minutes or until the apples are tender. Mash the pumpkin mixture, adding additional broth, if needed, until desired consistency.

Toasted Corn & Sage Harvest Risotto

MAKES 6 SERVINGS ■ **PREP:** 15 minutes ■ **COOK:** 35 minutes

- 1 **tablespoon olive oil**
- 1 **cup fresh *or* drained canned whole kernel corn**
- 1 **large orange *or* red pepper, chopped (about 1 cup)**
- 1 **medium onion, chopped (about ½ cup)**
- 1¾ **cups *uncooked* regular long-grain white rice**
- 4 **cups Swanson® Chicken Broth (Regular, Natural Goodness® *or* Certified Organic)**
- 1 **teaspoon ground sage**
- 1 **can (10¾ ounces) Campbell's® Condensed Cream of Celery Soup (Regular *or* 98% Fat Free)**
- ¼ **cup grated Parmesan cheese**

1. Heat the oil in a 4-quart saucepan over medium heat. Add the corn, pepper and onion and cook for 5 minutes or until the vegetables are lightly browned.

2. Add the rice to the saucepan and cook and stir for 30 seconds. Stir in the broth and sage and heat to a boil. Reduce the heat to low. Cover and cook for 20 minutes or until the rice is tender.

3. Stir in the soup. Cook for 2 minutes or until the rice mixture is hot. Sprinkle with the cheese.

KITCHEN TIP

*If you want a meatless side dish, substitute Swanson® Vegetable Broth (Regular **or** Certified Organic) for the Chicken Broth.*

Heavenly Sweet Potatoes

MAKES 8 SERVINGS ■ **PREP:** 10 minutes ■ **BAKE:** 20 minutes

	Vegetable cooking spray
1	**can (40 ounces) cut sweet potatoes in heavy syrup, drained**
¼	**teaspoon ground cinnamon**
⅛	**teaspoon ground ginger**
¾	**cup Swanson® Chicken Broth (Regular, Natural Goodness®** *or* **Certified Organic)**
2	**cups miniature marshmallows**

1. Heat the oven to 350°F.

2. Spray a 1½-quart casserole with cooking spray.

3. Put the potatoes, cinnamon and ginger in an electric mixer bowl. Beat at medium speed until almost smooth. Add the broth and beat until potatoes are fluffy. Spoon the potato mixture in the prepared dish. Top with the marshmallows.

4. Bake for 20 minutes or until heated through and marshmallows are golden brown.

Layered Cranberry Walnut Stuffing

MAKES 6 SERVINGS ■ **PREP:** 10 minutes ■ **BAKE:** 25 minutes

  2 **boxes (6 ounces *each*) Pepperidge Farm® Stuffing Mix**
1½ **cups Swanson® Chicken Broth (Regular, Natural Goodness®**
    ***or* Certified Organic)**
  2 **tablespoons butter**
  1 **can (16 ounces) whole cranberry sauce**
  ½ **cup walnuts, toasted and chopped**

1. Prepare the stuffing using the broth and butter according to the package directions.

2. Spoon **half** of the stuffing into a 2-quart casserole. Spoon **half** of the cranberry sauce over the stuffing. Sprinkle with ¼ **cup** walnuts. Repeat the layers.

3. Bake at 350°F. for 25 minutes or until hot.

■ **KITCHEN TIP**

The flavor and crispness of nuts come out when they're toasted, and the nuts are easier to chop when warm. Spread the nuts in a single layer on a baking sheet, then bake them in a preheated 350°F. oven for 10 minutes or until they're golden brown. Stir them occasionally so they toast evenly.

Broth Simmered Rice

MAKES 4 SERVINGS ■ **PREP:** 5 minutes ■ **COOK:** 25 minutes

1¾   **cups Swanson® Chicken Broth (Regular, Natural Goodness® *or* Certified Organic)**

¾   **cup *uncooked* regular long-grain white rice**

1. Heat the broth in a 2-quart saucepan over medium-high heat to a boil.

2. Stir in the rice. Reduce the heat to low. Cover and cook for 20 minutes or until the rice is tender.

KITCHEN TIP

This recipe will work with any variety of Swanson® Broth.

Florentine Simmered Rice: Add ***1 teaspoon*** dried Italian seasoning to broth. Add ***1 cup*** chopped spinach with rice. Stir in ½ ***cup*** grated Parmesan cheese before serving. Serve with additional cheese.

Ultra Creamy Mashed Potatoes

MAKES 6 SERVINGS ■ **PREP:** 15 minutes ■ **COOK:** 20 minutes

3½ cups Swanson® Chicken Broth (Regular, Natural Goodness® *or* Certified Organic)

5 large potatoes, cut into 1-inch pieces (about 7½ cups)

½ cup light cream

2 tablespoons butter

Generous dash ground black pepper

1 can (14½ ounces) Campbell's® Turkey Gravy

1. Heat the broth and potatoes in a 3-quart saucepan over medium-high heat to a boil.

2. Reduce the heat to medium. Cover and cook for 10 minutes or until the potatoes are tender. Drain, reserving the broth.

3. Mash the potatoes with ¼ **cup** broth, cream, butter and black pepper. Add additional broth, if needed, until desired consistency. Serve with the gravy.

Ultimate Mashed Potatoes: Stir ½ **cup** sour cream, **3** slices bacon, cooked and crumbled (reserve some for garnish), and ¼ **cup** chopped fresh chives into the hot mashed potatoes. Sprinkle with the reserved bacon.

VOLUME MEASUREMENTS (dry)

$1/8$ teaspoon = 0.5 mL
$1/4$ teaspoon = 1 mL
$1/2$ teaspoon = 2 mL
$3/4$ teaspoon = 4 mL
1 teaspoon = 5 mL
1 tablespoon = 15 mL
2 tablespoons = 30 mL
$1/4$ cup = 60 mL
$1/3$ cup = 75 mL
$1/2$ cup = 125 mL
$2/3$ cup = 150 mL
$3/4$ cup = 175 mL
1 cup = 250 mL
2 cups = 1 pint = 500 mL
3 cups = 750 mL
4 cups = 1 quart = 1 L

VOLUME MEASUREMENTS (fluid)

1 fluid ounce (2 tablespoons) = 30 mL
4 fluid ounces ($1/2$ cup) = 125 mL
8 fluid ounces (1 cup) = 250 mL
12 fluid ounces ($1 1/2$ cups) = 375 mL
16 fluid ounces (2 cups) = 500 mL

WEIGHTS (mass)

$1/2$ ounce = 15 g
1 ounce = 30 g
3 ounces = 90 g
4 ounces = 120 g
8 ounces = 225 g
10 ounces = 285 g
12 ounces = 360 g
16 ounces = 1 pound = 450 g

DIMENSIONS

$1/16$ inch = 2 mm
$1/8$ inch = 3 mm
$1/4$ inch = 6 mm
$1/2$ inch = 1.5 cm
$3/4$ inch = 2 cm
1 inch = 2.5 cm

OVEN TEMPERATURES

250°F = 120°C
275°F = 140°C
300°F = 150°C
325°F = 160°C
350°F = 180°C
375°F = 190°C
400°F = 200°C
425°F = 220°C
450°F = 230°C

BAKING PAN AND DISH EQUIVALENTS

Utensil	Size in Inches	Size in Centimeters	Volume	Metric Volume
Baking or Cake Pan (square or rectangular)	8×8×2	20×20×5	8 cups	2 L
	9×9×2	23×23×5	10 cups	2.5 L
	13×9×2	33×23×5	12 cups	3 L
Loaf Pan	8½×4½×2½	21×11×6	6 cups	1.5 L
	9×9×3	23×13×7	8 cups	2 L
Round Layer Cake Pan	8×1½	20×4	4 cups	1 L
	9×1½	23×4	5 cups	1.25 L
Pie Plate	8×1½	20×4	4 cups	1 L
	9×1½	23×4	5 cups	1.25 L
Baking Dish or Casserole			1 quart/4 cups	1 L
			1½ quart/6 cups	1.5 L
			2 quart/8 cups	2 L
			3 quart/12 cups	3 L

Butternut Squash & Baby Spinach in a Savory Broth

Blue Cheese Potato Soup with Olive Tapenade

Butternut Squash & Baby Spinach in a Savory Broth

MAKES 8 SERVINGS ■ **PREP:** 20 minutes ■ **COOK:** 35 minutes

2 tablespoons butter
1 small onion, finely chopped (about ½ cup)
2 cloves garlic, minced
1 small butternut squash, peeled, seeded and diced (about 4½ cups)
2 large carrots, diced (about 1 cup)
6 cups Swanson® Chicken Broth (Regular, Natural Goodness® *or* Certified Organic)
¼ teaspoon ground cinnamon
1 bag (6 ounces) baby spinach leaves

1. Heat the butter in a 6-quart saucepot over medium-high heat. Add the onion and cook until it's tender. Add the garlic and cook for 30 seconds. Stir in the squash and carrots and cook for 5 minutes.

2. Stir in the broth and cinnamon and heat to a boil. Reduce the heat to low. Cover and cook for 10 minutes or until the vegetables are tender.

3. Stir in the spinach and cook until the spinach is wilted. Season to taste.

◼ KITCHEN TIP

Cooking the spinach just until it wilts in Step 3 helps it to maintain its vibrant green color.

Blue Cheese Potato Soup with Olive Tapenade

MAKES 12 SERVINGS ■ **PREP:** 25 minutes ■ **COOK:** 40 minutes

2 tablespoons olive oil
2 medium onions, chopped (about 1 cup)
5 cloves garlic, minced
6 cups Swanson® Vegetable Broth (Regular *or* Certified Organic)
4 pounds red potatoes, peeled and diced
1 tablespoon balsamic vinegar
⅓ cup crumbled blue cheese
½ cup prepared olive tapenade

1. Heat the oil in a 6-quart saucepot over medium heat. Add the onions and garlic and cook until they're tender.

2. Stir the broth and potatoes in the saucepot and heat to a boil. Reduce the heat to low. Cover and cook for 30 minutes or until the potatoes are tender.

3. Pour ⅓ of the broth mixture into a blender or food processor. Cover and blend until smooth. Pour the mixture into a large bowl. Repeat twice more with the remaining broth mixture. Return all of the puréed mixture to the saucepot. Stir in the vinegar and cheese. Increase the heat to medium. Cook for 5 minutes or until the mixture is hot and bubbling. Season as desired.

4. Divide the soup mixture among **12** serving bowls. Top **each** with **2 teaspoons** tapenade.

Twice-Baked Potato Soup

Slow-Simmered Chicken Rice Soup

Twice-Baked Potato Soup

MAKES 8 SERVINGS ■ **PREP:** 10 minutes ■ **COOK:** 45 minutes

6	large baking potatoes, scrubbed and pricked with a fork
2	tablespoons butter
1	small sweet onion, finely chopped (about ½ cup)
5	cups Swanson® Chicken Broth (Regular, Natural Goodness® *or* Certified Organic)
¼	cup light cream
1	tablespoon chopped fresh chives *Potato Toppers*

1. Heat the oven to 425°F. Arrange the potatoes on a rack and bake for 30 minutes or until tender. Place the potatoes in a bowl with a lid and let steam. Remove the skin and mash pulp.

2. Heat the butter in a 3-quart saucepan. Add the onion and cook until tender. Add the broth and **5 cups** of the potato pulp.

3. Place ⅓ of the broth mixture into an electric blender or food processor container. Cover and blend until smooth. Place in a medium bowl. Repeat the blending process with the remaining broth mixture. Return all of the puréed mixture into the saucepan. Stir in the cream and chives and cook for 5 minutes more. Season to taste.

4. Place ¼ **cup** of the remaining pulp mixture in **each** of **8** serving bowls. Divide the broth mixture among the bowls. Serve with one or more *Potato Toppers*.

Potato Toppers: Cooked crumbled bacon, shredded Cheddar cheese **and/or** sour cream.

■ KITCHEN TIP

Microwave the potatoes on HIGH for 10 to 12 minutes or until fork-tender.

Slow-Simmered Chicken Rice Soup

MAKES 8 SERVINGS ■ **PREP:** 10 minutes ■ **COOK:** 7 hours 15 minutes

½	cup *uncooked* wild rice
½	cup *uncooked* regular long-grain white rice
1	tablespoon vegetable oil
5¼	cups Swanson® Chicken Broth (Regular, Natural Goodness® *or* Certified Organic)
2	teaspoons dried thyme leaves, crushed
¼	teaspoon crushed red pepper
2	stalks celery, coarsely chopped (about 1 cup)
1	medium onion, chopped (about ½ cup)
1	pound skinless, boneless chicken breasts, cut into cubes
	Sour cream (optional)
	Chopped green onions (optional)

1. Stir the wild rice, white rice and oil in a 3½-quart slow cooker. Cover and cook on HIGH for 15 minutes.

2. Add the broth, thyme, red pepper, celery, onion and chicken to the cooker. Turn the heat to LOW. Cover and cook for 7 to 8 hours* or until the chicken is cooked through.

3. Serve with the sour cream and green onions, if desired.

Or on HIGH for 4 to 5 hours.

■ KITCHEN TIP

*Speed preparation by substituting **3 cans** (4.5 ounces **each**) Swanson® Premium Chunk Chicken Breast, drained, for the raw chicken.*

Roasted Vegetable Soup with Garlic Herb Drizzle

Thai Roasted Squash Soup

Roasted Vegetable Soup with Garlic Herb Drizzle

MAKES 8 SERVINGS ■ **PREP:** 15 minutes ■ **BAKE:** 25 minutes ■ **COOK:** 30 minutes

1	**small bulb garlic**
7	**tablespoons olive oil**
1	**pound white potatoes, cut into cubes**
1	**small bulb fennel, cut into cubes**
2	**carrots, chopped (about 1 cup)**
1	**medium sweet onion, chopped (about 1 cup)**
6	**cups Swanson® Vegetable Broth (Regular *or* Certified Organic)**
¼	**cup finely chopped fresh basil *and/or* parsley leaves**

1. Heat the oven to 425°F. Cut ⅓ off the top of the garlic bulb and discard. Place remaining garlic on a piece of aluminum foil. Drizzle with **1 tablespoon** of the olive oil and wrap. Arrange the potatoes, fennel, carrots and onion in a 17×11-inch roasting pan. Pour **2 tablespoons** of the oil over the vegetables and toss to coat. Season to taste. Bake the vegetables and garlic for 25 minutes.

2. Place **1 cup** of the broth with the vegetable mixture into an electric blender or food processor container. Cover and blend until coarsely puréed. Pour the mixture into a 3-quart saucepan.

3. Add the remaining broth. Cook over high heat to a boil. Reduce the heat to low. Cook for 5 minutes.

4. Meanwhile, peel and smash the garlic in a small bowl. Add the basil and remaining oil.

5. Divide the soup among **8** serving bowls. Top **each** with **about 1 tablespoon** of the herbed oil mixture.

Thai Roasted Squash Soup

MAKES 6 SERVINGS ■ **PREP:** 35 minutes ■ **COOK:** 50 minutes

2	**tablespoons vegetable oil**
2	**teaspoons curry powder**
1	**butternut squash, peeled, seeded and cut into 2-inch pieces (about 6 cups)**
1	**large sweet onion, cut into eighths**
1	**tablespoon chopped fresh ginger root**
3	**cups Swanson® Chicken Broth (Regular, Natural Goodness® *or* Certified Organic)**
1	**can (15 ounces) cream of coconut**
3	**tablespoons chopped fresh cilantro leaves**

1. Heat the oven to 425°F. Stir the oil and curry in a large bowl. Add the squash and onions and toss to coat. Spread the vegetables onto a 17×11-inch roasting pan.

2. Bake for 25 minutes until the vegetables are golden brown, stirring occasionally.

3. Heat the vegetables, ginger root, broth and cream of coconut in a 4-quart saucepan over medium-high heat to a boil. Reduce the heat to low. Cook for 20 minutes or until the vegetables are tender.

4. Spoon ⅓ of the vegetable mixture into a blender or food processor. Cover and blend until smooth. Pour the mixture into a large bowl. Repeat the blending process twice more with the remaining vegetable mixture. Return all of the puréed mixture to the saucepan. Cook over medium heat until the mixture is hot. Season to taste. Divide the soup among **6** serving bowls. Sprinkle with the cilantro.

Hearty Chicken Tortilla Soup

Madeira Mushroom and Leek Soup

Hearty Chicken Tortilla Soup

MAKES 6 SERVINGS ■ **PREP:** 10 minutes ■ **COOK:** 30 minutes

Vegetable cooking spray

4 skinless, boneless chicken breasts, cut into 1-inch pieces (about 1 pound)

3½ cups Swanson® Chicken Broth (Regular, Natural Goodness® or Certified Organic)

1 teaspoon ground cumin

½ cup *uncooked* regular long-grain white rice

1 can (11 ounces) whole kernel corn with red and green peppers, drained

1 cup Pace® Picante Sauce

1 tablespoon chopped fresh cilantro leaves

2 tablespoons fresh lime juice

Crisp Tortilla Strips

1. Spray a 6-quart saucepot with the cooking spray. Heat over medium-high heat for 1 minute. Add the chicken to the saucepot. Cook until it's browned, stirring often.

2. Stir the broth, cumin and rice in the saucepot. Heat to a boil. Reduce the heat to low. Cover and cook for 20 minutes.

3. Stir the corn, picante sauce, cilantro and lime juice in the saucepot. Cook until the rice is tender. Top **each** serving of soup with *Crisp Tortilla Strips*.

Crisp Tortilla Strips: Heat the oven to 425°F. Cut **4** corn tortillas into thin strips and place them on a baking sheet. Spray with the cooking spray. Bake for 10 minutes or until golden.

■ **KITCHEN TIP**

Use a pastry wheel when cutting the tortillas to create a special touch for the soup garnish.

Madeira Mushroom and Leek Soup

MAKES 6 SERVINGS ■ **PREP:** 10 minutes ■ **STAND:** 30 minutes ■ **COOK:** 1 hour 15 minutes

6 cups Swanson® Vegetable Broth (Regular *or* Certified Organic)

½ cup Madeira wine

1 ounce dried shiitake, morel *or* cépes mushrooms

4 tablespoons butter

3 leeks, white part only, coarsely chopped (about 2 cups)

2 tablespoons all-purpose flour

1 package (8 ounces) sliced white mushrooms (about 3 cups)

¼ teaspoon ground black pepper

Additional chopped mushrooms *and* chopped leeks

1. Heat **1 cup** broth, wine and dried mushrooms in a 1-quart saucepan over high heat to a boil. Remove the saucepan from the heat. Let stand for 30 minutes. Do not drain.

2. Heat the butter in a 4-quart saucepan over low heat. Add the leeks and cook until they're tender-crisp. Stir in the flour. Cook and stir for 5 minutes.

3. Gradually stir in the remaining broth, fresh mushrooms, black pepper and the dried mushroom mixture. Heat to a boil. Reduce the heat to low and cook for 30 minutes or until the mushrooms are tender.

4. Place ⅓ of the mushroom mixture into a blender or food processor. Cover and blend until the mixture is smooth. Pour the mixture into a large bowl. Repeat twice more with the remaining mushroom mixture. Return all the puréed mixture to the saucepan. Cook over medium heat for 5 minutes or until the mixture is hot and bubbling.

5. Divide the soup among **6** serving bowls. Garnish with the additional mushrooms and leeks.

Sensational Chicken Noodle Soup

Roasted Squash Soup with Crispy Bacon

Sensational Chicken Noodle Soup

MAKES 4 SERVINGS ■ **PREP:** 5 minutes ■ **COOK:** 25 minutes

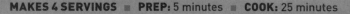

4 cups Swanson® Chicken Broth
  (Regular, Natural Goodness®
  or Certified Organic)
  Generous dash ground black pepper
1 medium carrot, sliced (about ½ cup)
1 stalk celery, sliced (about ½ cup)
½ cup *uncooked* extra wide egg noodles
1 cup shredded cooked chicken *or*
  turkey

1. Heat the broth, black pepper, carrot and celery in a 2-quart saucepan over medium-high heat to a boil.

2. Stir the noodles and chicken into the saucepan. Reduce the heat to medium. Cook for 10 minutes or until the noodles are tender.

Asian Soup: Add **2** green onions cut into ½-inch pieces, **1 clove** garlic, minced, **1 teaspoon** ground ginger and **2 teaspoons** soy sauce. Substitute **uncooked** curly Asian noodles for egg noodles.

Mexican Soup: Add ½ cup Pace® Chunky Salsa, **1 clove** garlic, minced, **1 cup** rinsed and drained black beans and ½ **teaspoon** chili powder. Substitute **2** corn tortillas (4 or 6-inch) cut into thin strips for the noodles, adding them just before serving.

Italian Tortellini Soup: Add **1 can** (about 14.5 ounces) diced tomatoes, drained, **1 clove** garlic, minced, **1 teaspoon** dried Italian seasoning, crushed and **1 cup** spinach leaves. Substitute ½ **cup** frozen cheese tortellini for egg noodles. Serve with grated Parmesan cheese.

Roasted Squash Soup with Crispy Bacon

MAKES 6 SERVINGS ■ **PREP:** 15 minutes ■ **BAKE:** 25 minutes ■ **COOK:** 5 minutes

1 small butternut squash (about
  1½ pounds), diced (about 4 cups)
2 large onions, sliced (about 2 cups)
3 tablespoons olive oil
3 cups Swanson® Chicken Broth
  (Regular, Natural Goodness®
  or Certified Organic)
½ cup heavy cream
¼ cup real bacon bits

1. Heat the oven to 425°F. Place the squash and onions in a 17×11-inch roasting pan. Add the oil and toss to coat. Bake for 25 minutes or until the squash is tender.

2. Place ½ of the squash mixture, **1½ cups** of the broth and ¼ **cup** of the cream in an electric blender or food processor container.

Cover and blend until smooth. Pour the mixture into a medium bowl. Repeat the blending process with the remaining squash mixture, broth and cream. Season to taste. Return all of the puréed mixture to a 3-quart saucepan. Cook over medium heat for 5 minutes or until hot.

3. Divide the soup among **6** serving bowls. Top **each** serving of soup with **2 teaspoons** of the bacon.

KITCHEN TIP

Ready-cut butternut squash is sold in 20-ounce bags in the produce section, or you may also find it in the frozen foods section of your supermarket.

Asian Chicken Noodle Soup

Roasted Chicken with Caramelized Onions Soup

Asian Chicken Noodle Soup

MAKES 4 SERVINGS ■ **PREP:** 5 minutes ■ **COOK:** 20 minutes

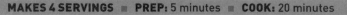

3½	cups Swanson® Chicken Broth (Regular, Natural Goodness® *or* Certified Organic)
1	teaspoon soy sauce
1	teaspoon ground ginger
	Generous dash ground black pepper
1	medium carrot, diagonally sliced
1	stalk celery, diagonally sliced
½	red pepper, cut into 2-inch-long strips
2	green onions, diagonally sliced
1	clove garlic, minced
½	cup broken-up *uncooked* curly Asian noodles
1	cup shredded cooked chicken

1. Heat the broth, soy sauce, ginger, black pepper, carrot, celery, red pepper, green onions and garlic in a 2-quart saucepan over medium-high heat to a boil.

2. Stir the noodles and chicken in the saucepan. Reduce the heat to medium and cook for 10 minutes or until the noodles are done.

For an Interesting Twist: Use **1 cup** sliced bok choy for the celery and **2 ounces uncooked** cellophane noodles for the curly Asian noodles. Reduce the cook time to 5 minutes.

Roasted Chicken with Caramelized Onions Soup

MAKES 6 SERVINGS ■ **PREP:** 10 minutes ■ **COOK:** 30 minutes

2	teaspoons vegetable oil
2	medium onions, cut in half and thinly sliced (about 1 cup)
8	cups Swanson® Chicken Broth (Regular, Natural Goodness® *or* Certified Organic)
⅛	teaspoon ground black pepper
2	medium carrots, sliced (about 1 cup)
2	stalks celery, sliced (about 1 cup)
¾	cup *uncooked* trumpet-shaped pasta (campanelle)
2	cups roasted chicken, cut into strips

1. Heat the oil in a 10-inch skillet over medium-high heat. Add the onions and cook until they begin to brown, stirring occasionally. Reduce the heat to medium. Cook until the onions are tender and caramelized, stirring occasionally. Remove the skillet from the heat.

2. Heat the broth, black pepper, carrots and celery in a 4-quart saucepan over medium-high heat to a boil. Stir the pasta and chicken in the saucepan. Reduce the heat to medium. Cook for 10 minutes or until the pasta is tender. Stir in the onions and serve immediately.

■ KITCHEN TIP

*Cut the peeled onions in half lengthwise. Place the halves cut-side down on the cutting surface. Slice **each** onion half in parallel cuts up to, but not through, the root. Cut the root end off to free the slices.*

Corn & Red Pepper Chowder

Crab and Corn Chowder

Corn & Red Pepper Chowder

MAKES 6 SERVINGS ■ **PREP:** 20 minutes ■ **COOK:** 45 minutes

2	tablespoons vegetable oil
1	large sweet onion, diced (about 1 cup)
¼	cup all-purpose flour
2	cloves garlic, minced
6	cups Swanson® Chicken Broth (Regular, Natural Goodness® *or* Certified Organic)
2	medium Yukon gold potatoes, diced (about 2 cups)
2	cups fresh whole kernel corn *or* 1 package (about 10 ounces) frozen whole kernel corn
1	jar (about 7 ounces) roasted red peppers, drained and chopped
½	cup heavy cream (optional)
⅓	cup chopped fresh basil leaves

1. Heat the oil in a 4-quart saucepan over medium heat. Add the onion and cook until it's tender. Stir in the flour and garlic. Cook and stir for 1 minute.

2. Stir the broth and potatoes in the saucepan. Heat to a boil. Reduce the heat to low and cook for 20 minutes or until the potatoes are tender.

3. Stir the corn and red peppers in the saucepan. Cook for 10 minutes.

4. Add the cream, if desired, and ¼ **cup** of the basil. Season to taste. Divide the soup among **6** serving bowls. Sprinkle **each** serving of soup with the remaining basil.

Crab and Corn Chowder

MAKES 6 SERVINGS ■ **PREP:** 15 minutes ■ **COOK:** 35 minutes

4	slices bacon
1	large sweet onion, coarsely chopped (about 1 cup)
2	cloves garlic, minced
6	cups Swanson® Chicken Broth (Regular, Natural Goodness® *or* Certified Organic)
2	teaspoons seafood seasoning
6	to 8 red potatoes *or* fingerling potatoes, cut into 1-inch pieces (about 2 cups)
2	cups frozen whole kernel corn
1	container (8 ounces) refrigerated pasteurized lump crabmeat
½	cup heavy cream

1. Cook the bacon in a 4-quart saucepan over medium-high heat for 5 minutes or until it's crisp. Remove the bacon with a fork or kitchen tongs and drain on paper towels. Crumble the bacon and set aside. Pour off all but **2 tablespoons** drippings.

2. Reduce the heat to medium. Add the onion and garlic to the saucepan and cook until the onion is tender.

3. Stir the broth, seafood seasoning, potatoes and corn in the saucepan. Heat to a boil. Reduce the heat to low and cook for 15 minutes or until the potatoes are tender.

4. Stir in the crabmeat and cream and cook for 5 minutes or until the mixture is hot and bubbling. Divide the chowder among **6** serving bowls. Top **each** with **about 1 tablespoon** bacon.

KITCHEN TIP

*If you can't find sweet onions, regular white **or** yellow onions will work in this recipe.*

Simply Special Seafood Chowder

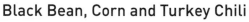

Black Bean, Corn and Turkey Chili

Simply Special Seafood Chowder

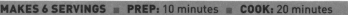

MAKES 6 SERVINGS ■ **PREP:** 10 minutes ■ **COOK:** 20 minutes

1 tablespoon olive oil *or* vegetable oil
1 medium bulb fennel, trimmed, halved and thinly sliced (about 2 cups)
1 medium onion, chopped (about ½ cup)
1 teaspoon dried thyme leaves, crushed
5 cups water
1¾ cups Swanson® Vegetable Broth (Regular *or* Certified Organic)
1 can (10¾ ounces) Campbell's® Condensed Tomato Soup
1 package (about 10 ounces) frozen whole baby carrots, thawed (about 1½ cups)
½ pound fresh *or* thawed frozen firm white fish fillet (cod, haddock *or* halibut), cut into 2-inch pieces

½ pound fresh large shrimp, peeled and deveined
¾ pound mussels (about 12), well scrubbed and beards removed
Freshly ground black pepper

1. Heat the oil in a 6-quart saucepot over medium heat. Add the fennel, onion and thyme and cook until they're tender. Stir the water, broth, soup and carrots in the saucepot and heat to a boil.

2. Add the fish. Cover and cook over medium heat for 2 minutes. Discard any open or cracked mussels. Add the shrimp and mussels. Cover and simmer for 3 minutes or until the fish flakes easily with a fork, the shrimp are pink and the mussels open. Discard any mussels that do not open. Sprinkle with black pepper.

Black Bean, Corn and Turkey Chili

MAKES 6 SERVINGS ■ **PREP:** 15 minutes ■ **COOK:** 40 minutes

1 tablespoon vegetable oil
1 pound ground turkey
1 large onion, chopped (about 1 cup)
2 tablespoons chili powder
1 teaspoon ground cumin
1 teaspoon dried oregano leaves, crushed
½ teaspoon ground black pepper
¼ teaspoon garlic powder *or* 2 cloves garlic, minced
1¾ cups Swanson® Chicken Stock
1 cup Pace® Picante Sauce
1 tablespoon sugar

1 can (about 15 ounces) black beans, rinsed and drained
1 can (about 16 ounces) whole kernel corn, drained

1. Heat the oil in a 4-quart saucepan over medium-high heat. Add the turkey, onion, chili powder, cumin, oregano, black pepper and garlic powder. Cook until the turkey is well browned, stirring often to separate meat.

2. Stir the stock, picante sauce, sugar, beans and corn in the saucepan and heat to a boil. Reduce the heat to low. Cover and cook for 30 minutes or until the mixture is hot and bubbling.

Poblano Corn Chowder with Chicken and Chorizo

Southwestern Chicken Chili

Poblano Corn Chowder with Chicken and Chorizo

MAKES 8 SERVINGS ■ **PREP:** 15 minutes ■ **COOK:** 8 hours

4 cups Swanson® Chicken Broth (Regular, Natural Goodness® *or* Certified Organic)

1 tablespoon sugar

2 cans (14.5 ounces *each*) cream-style corn

1 large potato, diced (about 2 cups)

2 large poblano chiles, seeded and diced (about 2 cups)

1 package (10 ounces) frozen whole kernel corn, thawed

1 pound skinless, boneless chicken (breasts *and/or* thighs), cut into cubes

½ pound chorizo sausage, diced

1 cup heavy cream

¼ cup chopped fresh cilantro

Place the broth, sugar, canned corn, potato, chiles, frozen corn, chicken and sausage in a 6-quart slow cooker. Cover and cook on LOW for 8 hours*. Stir in the cream and cilantro.

Or on HIGH for 4 hours.

KITCHEN TIP

*To enhance the flavor of the chowder, roast the chiles and corn before adding to the cooker. Place the chiles and thawed corn in a single layer in a roasting pan. Drizzle with **1 tablespoon** olive oil. Toss to coat. Bake at 375°F. for 30 minutes.*

Southwestern Chicken Chili

MAKES 6 SERVINGS ■ **PREP:** 15 minutes ■ **COOK:** 35 minutes

2 tablespoons olive oil

1 cup chopped onion

½ cup chopped celery

½ cup chopped red pepper

3 tablespoons all-purpose flour

1 tablespoon ground cumin

2 cups Swanson® Chicken Stock

2 cans (15 ounces *each*) great Northern beans

1 jar (16 ounces) Pace® Picante Sauce

2 cups chopped cooked chicken
Shredded Pepper Jack cheese
Cubed avocado

1. Heat the oil in a 4-quart saucepot over medium heat. Add the onion, celery and pepper and cook until they're tender. Stir in the flour and cumin and cook for 2 minutes. Stir the stock in the saucepot. Cook and stir until the mixture boils.

2. Stir the beans, picante sauce and chicken in the saucepot. Heat to a boil. Reduce the heat to low. Cook for 20 minutes.

3. Garnish with the cheese and avocado.

Citrus Balsamic Salmon

Savory Orange Chicken with Sage

Citrus Balsamic Salmon

MAKES 8 SERVINGS ■ **PREP:** 10 minutes ■ **BAKE:** 15 minutes ■ **COOK:** 5 minutes

8	salmon fillets, ¾-inch thick
	Ground black pepper
3	tablespoons olive oil
1¾	cups Swanson® Chicken Stock
3	tablespoons balsamic vinegar
1½	tablespoons cornstarch
1	tablespoon orange juice
1	tablespoon packed brown sugar
1	teaspoon grated orange zest
	Orange slices

1. Season the salmon with the black pepper. Place the salmon into a 2-quart shallow baking dish. Drizzle with the olive oil. Bake at 350°F. for 15 minutes or until the salmon flakes easily when tested with a fork.

2. Heat the stock, vinegar, cornstarch, orange juice, brown sugar and orange zest in a 2-quart saucepan over medium-high heat to a boil. Cook and stir until the mixture boils and thickens.

3. Serve the salmon with the citrus sauce. Garnish with the orange slices.

KITCHEN TIP

Salmon and sauce may be refrigerated separately and served chilled.

Savory Orange Chicken with Sage

MAKES 4 SERVINGS ■ **PREP:** 10 minutes ■ **COOK:** 20 minutes

4	skinless, boneless chicken breasts halves (about 1 pound)
½	cup all-purpose flour
1	tablespoon vegetable oil
1	tablespoon butter
1¾	cups Swanson® Chicken Stock
⅓	cup orange juice
¼	cup Chablis *or* other dry white wine
1	tablespoon grated orange zest
1	tablespoon chopped fresh sage leaves *or* 1 teaspoon ground sage
¼	teaspoon ground black pepper
2	cups chopped shiitake mushrooms (about 3½ ounces)
	Hot cooked rice

1. Coat the chicken with the flour.

2. Heat the oil and butter in a 12-inch skillet over medium-high heat. Add the chicken and cook for 10 minutes or until it's well browned on both sides. Remove the chicken from the skillet.

3. Stir the stock, juice, wine, orange zest, sage and black pepper in the skillet and heat to a boil. Stir in the mushrooms. Return the chicken to the skillet. Reduce the heat to low. Cook for 5 minutes or until the chicken is cooked through and liquid is reduced by one-fourth. Serve with the rice.

Almond-Crusted Salmon with Thyme & Lemon Butter Sauce

Holiday Brisket with Savory Onion Jus

Almond-Crusted Salmon with Thyme & Lemon Butter Sauce

MAKES 8 SERVINGS ▪ **PREP:** 15 minutes ▪ **BAKE:** 15 minutes

¼   **cup plain dry bread crumbs**
¼   **cup blanched almonds**
1   **clove garlic**
2   **tablespoons olive oil**
8   **salmon fillets (about 3 pounds)**
1   **tablespoon cornstarch**
1½ **cups Swanson® Chicken Stock**
2   **tablespoons lemon juice**
1   **teaspoon chopped fresh thyme leaves** *or* ¼ **teaspoon dried thyme leaves, crushed**
3   **tablespoons butter**
¼   **cup chopped shallot** *or* **onion**

1. Place the bread crumbs, almonds and garlic into a food processor or blender. Cover and process until the mixture is finely ground. Gradually pour in the olive oil while the food processor is running and process until the mixture is moist.

2. Place the salmon into a roasting pan. Top the salmon with the bread crumb mixture and press to adhere.

3. Bake at 400°F. for 15 minutes or until the salmon flakes easily when tested with a fork and the bread crumb mixture is golden. Remove the salmon from the oven and keep warm.

4. Stir the cornstarch, stock, lemon juice and thyme in a medium bowl until the mixture is smooth.

5. Heat **2 tablespoons** butter in a 1-quart saucepan over medium heat. Add the shallots and cook until they're tender. Stir in the cornstarch mixture and heat to a boil. Cook and stir until the sauce boils and thickens. Add the remaining butter and cook and stir until it's melted. Serve the salmon with the sauce.

Holiday Brisket with Savory Onion Jus

MAKES 8 SERVINGS ▪ **PREP:** 15 minutes ▪ **COOK:** 3 hours 15 minutes ▪ **STAND:** 10 minutes

2   **tablespoons olive** *or* **vegetable oil**
6   **medium onions, cut into quarters (about 6 cups)**
1   **medium butternut squash (about 3 pounds), peeled, seeded and cut into 1½-inch cubes (about 6 cups)**
    3-pound boneless beef brisket
1¾ **cups Swanson® Beef Stock**
½   **cup orange juice**
½   **cup dry red wine**
½   **cup packed brown sugar**
1   **can (about 28 ounces) whole peeled tomatoes**

1. Heat the oil in an 8-quart saucepot over medium-high heat. Add the onions and squash and cook over medium heat until they're tender-crisp. Remove the vegetables from the saucepot.

2. Season the beef as desired. Increase the heat to medium-high. Add the beef to the saucepot and cook until it's well browned on both sides. Remove the beef from the saucepot. Pour off any fat.

3. Add the stock, orange juice, wine, brown sugar and tomatoes to the saucepot and heat to a boil. Reduce the heat to low. Return the beef to the saucepot. Cover and cook for 2 hours.

4. Return the vegetables to the saucepot. Cover and cook for 1 hour or until the beef is fork-tender.

5. Remove the beef to a cutting board. Let stand for 10 minutes. Serve the beef with the vegetables and sauce.

Rosemary Lamb Chops with Lemon Sauce

Savory Chicken Thighs with Figs

Rosemary Lamb Chops with Lemon Sauce

MAKES 3 SERVINGS ■ **PREP:** 5 minutes ■ **COOK:** 15 minutes

6　lamb chops (about ¾-inch thick)
1　teaspoon dried rosemary leaves, crushed
1　cup Swanson® Chicken Stock
2　teaspoons cornstarch
1　teaspoon lemon zest
3　tablespoons lemon juice
3　teaspoons Dijon-style mustard

1. Heat the broiler. Season the lamb with the rosemary. Place the lamb on a broiler pan.

2. Broil for 10 minutes (for medium-rare) or to desired doneness, turning the lamb over once halfway through broiling.

3. Stir the stock and cornstarch in a 1-quart saucepan until the mixture is smooth. Stir in the lemon zest, lemon juice and mustard. Cook and stir over medium heat until the mixture boils and thickens. Serve the stock mixture with the lamb.

KITCHEN TIP

The lamb chops can also be grilled. Lightly oil the grill rack and heat the grill to medium. Grill the lamb for 10 minutes (for medium-rare) or to desired doneness, turning the lamb over once halfway through grilling. Serve with the stock mixture.

Savory Chicken Thighs with Figs

MAKES 6 SERVINGS ■ **PREP:** 10 minutes ■ **COOK:** 30 minutes

1½　pounds boneless chicken thighs
2　tablespoons all-purpose flour
1　tablespoon olive oil
1　medium onion, chopped (about ½ cup)
3　cloves garlic, minced
1　cup Swanson® Chicken Stock
2　tablespoons balsamic vinegar
1　teaspoon dried thyme leaves, crushed
¼　teaspoon ground black pepper
6　ounces dried figs, stems removed and cut in half
　Hot cooked rice

1. Coat the chicken with the flour.

2. Heat the oil in a 10-inch skillet over medium-high heat. Add the chicken in 2 batches and cook until it's well browned on both sides.

3. Add the onion and garlic to the skillet and cook until the onion is tender. Stir the stock, vinegar, thyme, black pepper and figs in the skillet and heat to a boil. Reduce the heat to low. Cover and cook for 10 minutes or until the chicken is cooked through. Serve with the rice.

KITCHEN TIP

Chicken thighs are an inexpensive ingredient that can taste rich and decadent. The balsamic vinegar and figs in this recipe perfectly balance the richness of the chicken.

Spiral Ham with Mango Salsa

Roast Pork with Green Apples & Golden Squash

Spiral Ham with Mango Salsa

MAKES 24 SERVINGS ■ **PREP:** 30 minutes ■ **BAKE:** 2 hours

1	tablespoon butter
1	large onion, chopped (about 1 cup)
1½	cups Swanson® Chicken Stock
1	can (12 ounces) mango juice *or* nectar
1	package (4 ounces) dried mango, coarsely chopped
⅓	cup packed brown sugar
4	medium green onions, chopped (about ½ cup)
	9-pound fully-cooked bone-in *or* 6-pound fully-cooked boneless spiral cut ham

1. Heat the butter in a 2-quart saucepan over medium-high heat. Add the onion and cook until it's tender. Stir in the stock, mango juice, dried mango and brown sugar and heat to a boil. Reduce the heat to low. Cook and stir for 10 minutes or until the mixture boils and thickens. Remove the saucepan from the heat and let the mixture cool slightly.

2. Place a strainer over a medium bowl. Pour the stock mixture through the strainer. Reserve the stock mixture for the glaze. Place the strained mango mixture into a small bowl. Stir in the green onions. Cover the bowl and refrigerate until serving time.

3. Place the ham in a 17×11-inch roasting pan and cover loosely with foil. Bake at 325°F. for 1½ hours. Remove the foil. Spoon the reserved stock mixture over the ham. Bake for 30 minutes more or until the internal temperature of the ham reaches 140°F., basting the ham frequently with the pan drippings. Serve the ham with the mango salsa.

KITCHEN TIP

Substitute chopped fresh cilantro leaves for the green onions.

Roast Pork with Green Apples & Golden Squash

MAKES 8 SERVINGS ■ **PREP:** 20 minutes ■ **COOK:** 45 minutes

	Vegetable cooking spray
2	(¾ pound *each*) whole pork tenderloins
1	teaspoon olive oil
¼	teaspoon coarsely ground black pepper
3	large Granny Smith apples, cored and thickly sliced
1	butternut squash (about 1½ pounds), peeled, seeded and cut into cubes
2	tablespoons packed brown sugar
½	teaspoon ground cinnamon
1	medium onion, chopped (about ½ cup)
1¾	cups Swanson® Chicken Stock
2	teaspoons all-purpose flour

1. Heat the oven to 425°F. Spray a roasting pan with the cooking spray.

2. Brush the pork with the oil and season with the black pepper. Place the pork in the pan. Stir the apples, squash, brown sugar, cinnamon, onion and ½ **cup** stock in a large bowl. Add the apple mixture to the pan.

3. Roast for 25 minutes or until the pork is cooked through, stirring the apple mixture once during roasting. Remove the pork from the pan and keep it warm. Roast the apple mixture for 15 minutes or until it's browned. Remove the apple mixture from the pan.

4. Stir the remaining stock and flour in a small bowl until the mixture is smooth. Stir the stock mixture in the pan. Cook and stir over medium-high heat until the mixture boils and thickens, scraping up the browned bits from the bottom of the pan. Serve the stock mixture with the pork and apple mixture.

Beef Bourguignonne

Braised Beef with Shallots and Mushrooms

Beef Bourguignonne

MAKES 4 SERVINGS ■ **PREP:** 10 minutes ■ **COOK:** 30 minutes

1	beef sirloin steak *or* top round steak (about 1 pound), cut into 1-inch pieces
¼	cup all-purpose flour
1	tablespoon olive oil
1	medium onion, chopped (about ½ cup)
2	cloves garlic, minced
⅛	teaspoon dried parsley flakes
¼	teaspoon ground black pepper
2	cups sliced mushrooms (about 6 ounces)
1	teaspoon dried thyme leaves, crushed
2	cups fresh *or* frozen whole baby carrots
1¾	cups Swanson® Beef Stock
½	cup Burgundy *or* other dry red wine Hot cooked orzo pasta

1. Coat the beef with the flour.

2. Heat the oil in a 10-inch skillet over medium-high heat. Add the beef and cook until it's well browned, stirring often. Add the onion, garlic, parsley, black pepper, mushrooms and thyme and cook until the mushrooms are tender.

3. Stir the carrots, stock and wine in the skillet and heat to a boil. Reduce the heat to low. Cover and cook for 20 minutes or until the beef is cooked through. Serve the beef mixture over the orzo.

Braised Beef with Shallots and Mushrooms

MAKES 4 SERVINGS ■ **PREP:** 20 minutes ■ **COOK:** 2 hours 35 minutes

1	beef chuck pot roast, cut into serving-sized pieces (about 1½ pounds)
¼	cup all-purpose flour
3	tablespoons butter
½	pound small shallots, peeled
1	cup Swanson® Beef Stock
2	medium tomatoes, chopped (about 2 cups)
3	tablespoons balsamic vinegar
1	tablespoon packed brown sugar
2	large carrots, cut into 2-inch pieces (about 1 cup)
2	cups mushrooms, cut into quarters (about 5 ounces)
¼	cup chopped fresh parsley
2	tablespoons grated lemon zest

1. Coat the beef with the flour. Heat the butter in a 12-inch skillet over medium-high heat.

Add the beef and cook until it's well browned on all sides. Remove the beef from the skillet. Pour off any fat.

2. Add the shallots to the skillet. Cook for 10 minutes or until they're tender. Stir in the stock, tomatoes, vinegar and brown sugar and heat to a boil. Return the beef to the skillet. Reduce the heat to low. Cover and cook for 1½ hours.

3. Add the carrots and mushrooms to the skillet and cook for 30 minutes or until the beef is fork-tender and the vegetables are tender. Remove the beef and vegetables from the skillet and keep warm.

4. Increase the heat to high. Cook for 10 minutes or until the stock mixture is thickened. Return the beef and vegetables to the skillet. Season as desired. Sprinkle with the parsley and lemon zest.

Pork Chops with Cranberry Balsamic Sauce

Herb Roasted Turkey with Pan Gravy

Pork Chops with Cranberry Balsamic Sauce

MAKES 4 SERVINGS ■ **PREP:** 5 minutes ■ **COOK:** 30 minutes

4	boneless pork chops, 1-inch thick
	Lemon pepper seasoning
2	tablespoons butter
2	cloves garlic, thinly sliced
1¾	cups Swanson® Chicken Stock
¼	cup balsamic vinegar
½	cup dried cranberries *or* dried cherries

1. Season the pork with the lemon pepper. Cook the pork in a 10-inch nonstick skillet over medium heat for 20 minutes or until it's well browned on both sides and cooked through. Remove the pork from the skillet and keep warm.

2. Heat **1 tablespoon** butter in the skillet. Add the garlic and cook until it's tender. Stir the stock, vinegar and cranberries in the skillet and heat to a boil. Cook for 10 minutes or until the sauce is slightly thickened.

3. Stir in the remaining butter. Serve the pork with the sauce.

Herb Roasted Turkey with Pan Gravy

MAKES 12 SERVINGS ■ **PREP:** 15 minutes ■ **COOK:** 4 hours 20 minutes ■ **STAND:** 10 minutes

1¾	cups Swanson® Chicken Stock
3	tablespoons lemon juice
1	teaspoon dried basil leaves, crushed
1	teaspoon dried thyme leaves, crushed
⅛	teaspoon ground black pepper
1	(12- to 14-pound) turkey
¼	cup all-purpose flour

1. Stir the stock, lemon juice, basil, thyme and black pepper in a small bowl.

2. Roast the turkey according to the package directions, basting occasionally with the stock mixture during cooking. Let the turkey stand for 10 minutes before slicing.

3. Remove the turkey from the roasting pan. Spoon off any fat.

4. Stir the remaining stock mixture and flour in a small bowl until the mixture is smooth. Add the stock mixture to the roasting pan. Cook and stir over medium heat until the mixture boils and thickens. Serve the turkey with the gravy.

Sausage and Bean Ragoût

Cavatelli with Sausage & Broccoli

Sausage and Bean Ragoût

MAKES 6 SERVINGS ■ **PREP:** 15 minutes ■ **COOK:** 40 minutes

2	tablespoons olive oil
1	pound ground beef
1	pound hot Italian pork sausage, casing removed
1	large onion, chopped (about 1 cup)
4	cloves garlic, minced
3½	cups Swanson® Chicken Stock
¼	cup chopped fresh basil leaves
2	cans (14.5 ounces *each*) Italian-style diced tomatoes
1	can (about 15 ounces) white kidney beans (cannellini), rinsed and drained
½	cup *uncooked* elbow pasta
1	bag (6 ounces) fresh baby spinach leaves
⅓	cup grated Romano cheese

1. Heat the oil in a 6-quart saucepot over medium-high heat. Add the beef, sausage and onion and cook until the beef and sausage are well browned, stirring often to separate meat. Pour off any fat. Add the garlic and cook and stir for 30 seconds.

2. Stir the stock, basil, tomatoes and beans in the saucepot and heat to a boil. Reduce the heat to low. Cover and cook for 10 minutes, stirring occasionally. Add the pasta and cook until it's tender.

3. Stir in the spinach and cook until the spinach is wilted. Remove the saucepot from the heat and stir in the cheese. Serve with additional cheese, if desired.

KITCHEN TIP

This recipe calls for cooking the pasta until it's tender. However, if you like your pasta a little al dente, that will work as well.

Cavatelli with Sausage & Broccoli

MAKES 6 SERVINGS ■ **PREP:** 10 minutes ■ **COOK:** 30 minutes

1	package (1 pound) *uncooked* frozen narrow shell-shaped (cavatelli) pasta (about 3 cups)
1	tablespoon olive oil
1	pound sweet Italian pork sausage, casing removed
1	tablespoon butter
2	cloves garlic, minced
1	bag (about 16 ounces) frozen broccoli flowerets, thawed
2	cups Swanson® Chicken Stock
2	tablespoons grated Romano cheese Crushed red pepper flakes

1. Cook the pasta according to the package directions in a 6-quart saucepot. Drain the pasta well in a colander. Return the pasta to the saucepot.

2. Heat the oil in a 10-inch skillet over medium-high heat. Add the sausage and cook until it's well browned, stirring often to separate meat. Remove the sausage from the skillet. Pour off any fat.

3. Add the butter and garlic to the skillet. Reduce the heat to medium. Cook for 2 minutes or until the garlic is golden.

4. Add the broccoli to the skillet and cook for 5 minutes or until it's tender-crisp, stirring often. Stir in the stock and heat to a boil.

5. Add the broccoli mixture, sausage and cheese to the saucepot. Cook over medium heat for 10 minutes or until the stock mixture is thickened, stirring occasionally. Serve with the red pepper and additional cheese, if desired.

Easy One-Pot Spaghetti & Clams

Chicken Cacciatore & Pasta

Easy One-Pot Spaghetti & Clams

MAKES 8 SERVINGS ■ **PREP:** 5 minutes ■ **COOK:** 20 minutes

3	tablespoons olive oil
3	cloves garlic, minced
¼	teaspoon crushed red pepper flakes
8	cups Swanson® Chicken Stock
1	can (6.5 ounces) chopped clams, undrained
1	package (1 pound) *uncooked* thin spaghetti
1	can (10 ounces) whole baby clams, undrained
16	littleneck clams, scrubbed
⅓	cup chopped fresh parsley

1. Heat the oil in a 4-quart saucepan over medium heat. Add the garlic and red pepper. Cook for 1 minute. Add the stock and chopped clams. Heat to a boil.

2. Add the spaghetti. Cook for about 9 minutes or until the stock is absorbed. Add the canned and fresh clams. Cook for 2 minutes or until the fresh clams open. Toss with the parsley.

■ KITCHEN TIP

If using fresh clams, the shells should be tightly closed. If the shells are open, tap them slightly and if they don't close shut, then the clam is no longer alive and should be discarded. Also, after cooking discard any clams that do not open.

Chicken Cacciatore & Pasta

MAKES 4 SERVINGS ■ **PREP:** 10 minutes ■ **COOK:** 30 minutes

1	tablespoon vegetable oil
4	skinless, boneless chicken breast halves (about 1 pound)
1¾	cups Swanson® Chicken Stock
1	teaspoon dried oregano leaves, crushed
1	teaspoon garlic powder
1	can (14.5 ounces) diced tomatoes
1	small green pepper, cut into 2-inch-long strips (about 1 cup)
1	medium onion, cut into wedges
¼	teaspoon ground black pepper
2½	cups *uncooked* medium shell-shaped pasta

1. Heat the oil in a 10-inch skillet over medium-high heat. Add the chicken and cook for 10 minutes or until it's well browned on both sides.

2. Stir the stock, oregano, garlic powder, tomatoes, green pepper, onion and black pepper in the skillet and heat to a boil. Stir in the pasta. Reduce the heat to low. Cover and cook for 15 minutes or until the pasta is tender.

Hearty Beef Stew

Greek-Style Beef Stew

Hearty Beef Stew

MAKES 4 SERVINGS ■ **PREP:** 15 minutes ■ **COOK:** 2 hours 15 minutes

1	**pound beef for stew, cut into 1-inch pieces**
3	**tablespoons all-purpose flour**
2	**tablespoons olive oil**
2	**cloves garlic, minced**
1¾	**cups Swanson® Beef Stock**
2	**medium onions, cut into quarters**
1	**bay leaf**
½	**teaspoon dried thyme leaves, crushed**
¼	**teaspoon ground black pepper**
2	**cups whole baby carrots**
2	**medium potatoes, cut into 2-inch pieces**
¼	**cup water**

1. Season the beef as desired. Coat with **1 tablespoon** flour. Heat the oil in a 6-quart saucepot over medium-high heat. Add the beef and cook until it's well browned, stirring often. Add the garlic to the saucepot and cook and stir for 1 minute.

2. Stir the stock, onions, bay leaf, thyme and black pepper in the saucepot and heat to a boil. Reduce the heat to low. Cover and cook for 1½ hours.

3. Add the carrots and potatoes to the saucepot. Cover and cook for 30 minutes or until the beef is fork-tender and the vegetables are tender. Remove and discard the bay leaf.

4. Stir the remaining flour and water in a small bowl until the mixture is smooth. Stir the flour mixture in the saucepot. Increase the heat to medium. Cook and stir until the mixture boils and thickens.

Greek-Style Beef Stew

MAKES 6 SERVINGS ■ **PREP:** 10 minutes ■ **COOK:** 8 hours

1	**boneless beef bottom round roast *or* chuck pot roast (about 2 pounds), cut into 1-inch pieces**
1	**bag (16 ounces) frozen whole small white onions**
1	**bag (16 ounces) fresh *or* frozen whole baby carrots**
2	**tablespoons all-purpose flour**
1¾	**cups Swanson® Beef Stock**
1	**can (5.5 ounces) V8® 100% Vegetable Juice**
1	**tablespoon packed brown sugar**
	Bouquet Garni
	Hot buttered noodles

1. Place the beef, onions and carrots into a 4-quart slow cooker. Sprinkle with the flour and toss to coat.

2. Stir the stock, vegetable juice and brown sugar in a medium bowl until the mixture is smooth. Pour the stock mixture over the beef and vegetables. Submerge the *Bouquet Garni* into the stock mixture.

3. Cover and cook on LOW for 8 to 9 hours* or until the beef is fork-tender. Remove the *Bouquet Garni*. Serve the beef mixture over the noodles.

Or on HIGH for 4 to 5 hours.

Bouquet Garni: Lay a 4-inch square of cheesecloth flat on the counter. Place ½ **teaspoon** whole cloves, **1** cinnamon stick and **1** bay leaf in the center of the cloth. Bring the corners of the cloth together and tie with kitchen string into a bundle.

Pork Chop Skillet Dinner

Herb-Simmered Beef Stew

Pork Chop Skillet Dinner

SWANSON

MAKES 4 SERVINGS ■ **PREP:** 10 minutes ■ **COOK:** 40 minutes

1	tablespoon olive oil
4	bone-in pork chops, ¾-inch thick *each*
1	medium onion, chopped (about ½ cup)
1	cup *uncooked* regular long-grain white rice
1¼	cups Swanson® Chicken Stock
1	cup orange juice
3	tablespoons chopped fresh parsley
¼	teaspoon ground black pepper
4	orange slices

1. Heat the oil in a 12-inch skillet over medium-high heat. Add the pork and cook until it's well browned on both sides.

2. Add the onion and rice to the skillet. Cook until the rice is lightly browned.

3. Stir in the stock, orange juice, **2 tablespoons** parsley and black pepper and heat to a boil. Reduce the heat to low. Cover and cook for 20 minutes or until the pork is cooked through and the rice is tender. Top with the orange slices and sprinkle with the remaining parsley.

Herb-Simmered Beef Stew

SWANSON

MAKES 6 SERVINGS ■ **PREP:** 15 minutes ■ **COOK:** 1 hour 30 minutes

2	pounds beef for stew, cut into 1-inch cubes
	Ground black pepper
2	tablespoons all-purpose flour
2	tablespoons olive oil
3	cups thickly-sliced mushrooms (about 8 ounces)
3	cloves garlic, minced
½	teaspoon dried marjoram leaves, crushed *or* 1½ teaspoons fresh marjoram leaves
½	teaspoon dried thyme leaves, crushed *or* 1½ teaspoons fresh thyme leaves
½	teaspoon dried rosemary leaves, crushed *or* 1½ teaspoons fresh rosemary leaves
1	bay leaf
1¾	cups Swanson® Beef Stock
3	cups fresh *or* frozen whole baby carrots
12	whole small red potatoes

1. Season the beef with the black pepper. Coat the beef with the flour.

2. Heat the oil in a 6-quart saucepot over medium-high heat. Add the beef in 2 batches and cook until it's well browned, stirring often. Pour off any fat.

3. Add the mushrooms, garlic, herbs and bay leaf to the saucepot and cook until the mushrooms are tender. Stir in the stock and heat to a boil. Reduce the heat to low. Cover and cook for 45 minutes.

4. Increase the heat to medium-high. Stir in the carrots and potatoes and heat to a boil. Reduce the heat to low. Cover and cook for 30 minutes or until the beef is fork-tender. Remove and discard the bay leaf.

Beef Teriyaki

Pan-Sautéed Chicken with Vegetables & Herbs

Beef Teriyaki

MAKES 4 SERVINGS ■ **PREP:** 10 minutes ■ **COOK:** 15 minutes

2	tablespoons cornstarch
1¾	cups Swanson® Beef Stock
2	tablespoons soy sauce
1	tablespoon packed brown sugar
½	teaspoon garlic powder
1	boneless beef sirloin steak
4	cups fresh *or* frozen broccoli flowerets
	Hot cooked rice

1. Stir the cornstarch, stock, soy sauce, brown sugar and garlic powder in a small bowl until the mixture is smooth.

2. Stir-fry the beef in a 10-inch nonstick skillet over medium-high heat until it's well browned, stirring often. Pour off any fat.

3. Add the broccoli to the skillet and cook for 1 minute. Stir in the cornstarch mixture. Cook and stir until the mixture boils and thickens. Serve the beef mixture over the rice.

KITCHEN TIP

To make slicing easier, freeze the beef for 1 hour before slicing.

Pan-Sautéed Chicken with Vegetables & Herbs

MAKES 4 SERVINGS ■ **PREP:** 20 minutes ■ **COOK:** 1 hour

⅛	teaspoon ground black pepper
⅛	teaspoon paprika
2	tablespoons all-purpose flour
4	bone-in chicken breast halves (about 2 pounds)
2	tablespoons olive oil
2	small red onions, cut into quarters
1	pound new potatoes, cut into quarters
8	ounces fresh whole baby carrots (about 16), green tops trimmed to 1-inch-long
1½	cups Swanson® Chicken Stock
3	tablespoons lemon juice
1	tablespoon chopped fresh oregano leaves
	Chopped fresh thyme leaves (optional)

1. Heat the oven to 350°F. Stir the black pepper, paprika and flour on a plate. Coat the chicken with the flour mixture.

2. Heat the oil in a 12-inch oven-safe skillet over medium-high heat. Add the chicken and cook until it's well browned on all sides. Remove the chicken from the skillet.

3. Add the onions and potatoes to the skillet and cook for 5 minutes. Add the carrots, stock, lemon juice and oregano and heat to a boil. Return the chicken to the skillet. Cover the skillet.

4. Bake for 20 minutes. Uncover the skillet and bake for 15 minutes or until the chicken is cooked through and the vegetables are tender. Sprinkle with the thyme, if desired.

Harvest Fruit Stuffing

Roasted Asparagus with Lemon & Goat Cheese

Harvest Fruit Stuffing

MAKES 8 SERVINGS ■ **PREP:** 10 minutes ■ **COOK:** 10 minutes ■ **BAKE:** 20 minutes

1¾ **cups Swanson® Chicken Broth (Regular, Natural Goodness® *or* Certified Organic)**
¼ **cup apple juice**
1 **cup cut-up mixed dried fruit**
1 **stalk celery, sliced (about ½ cup)**
1 **medium onion, chopped (about ½ cup)**
5 **cups Pepperidge Farm® Herb Seasoned Stuffing**

1. Heat the oven to 350°F.

2. Stir the broth, apple juice, dried fruit, celery and onion in a 3-quart saucepan. Heat to a boil over medium-high heat. Reduce the heat to low. Cover and cook for 5 minutes or until the vegetables are tender. Remove the saucepan from the heat. Add the stuffing and stir lightly to coat.

3. Spoon the stuffing into 1½-quart casserole. Bake for 20 minutes or until it's hot.

Roasted Asparagus with Lemon & Goat Cheese

MAKES 6 SERVINGS ■ **PREP:** 10 minutes ■ **COOK:** 20 minutes

Vegetable cooking spray
2 **pounds asparagus, trimmed**
1 **tablespoon olive oil**
Freshly ground black pepper
½ **cup Swanson® Vegetable Broth**
3 **ounces soft goat cheese, crumbled**
1 **tablespoon lemon juice**
1 **teaspoon grated lemon peel**

1. Heat the oven to 425°F. Spray a 17×11-inch roasting pan or shallow baking sheet with the cooking spray.

2. Stir the asparagus and oil in the pan. Season with the black pepper. Pour in the broth.

3. Roast the asparagus for 20 minutes or until it's tender, stirring once during cooking. Top with the cheese, lemon juice and lemon peel.

Pumpkin Apple Mash

Toasted Corn & Sage Harvest Risotto

Pumpkin Apple Mash

MAKES 4 SERVINGS ■ **PREP:** 10 minutes ■ **COOK:** 20 minutes

2   tablespoons butter
1   small onion, chopped (about ¼ cup)
¾   cup Swanson® Chicken Broth (Regular, Natural Goodness® or Certified Organic)
1   tablespoon packed brown sugar
¼   teaspoon dried thyme leaves, crushed
⅛   teaspoon ground black pepper
1   pumpkin or calabaza squash (about 2½ pounds), peeled, seeded and cut into 1-inch pieces (about 5 to 6 cups)
2   medium McIntosh apples, peeled, cored and cut into 1-inch pieces

1. Heat the butter in a 4-quart saucepan over medium-high heat. Add the onion and cook until the onion is tender-crisp.

2. Stir the broth, brown sugar, thyme, black pepper and pumpkin in the saucepan and heat to a boil. Reduce the heat to low. Cover and cook for 10 minutes or until the pumpkin is tender.

3. Stir the apples in the saucepan. Cook for 5 minutes or until the apples are tender. Mash the pumpkin mixture, adding additional broth, if needed, until desired consistency.

Toasted Corn & Sage Harvest Risotto

MAKES 6 SERVINGS ■ **PREP:** 15 minutes ■ **COOK:** 35 minutes

1   tablespoon olive oil
1   cup fresh or drained canned whole kernel corn
1   large orange or red pepper, chopped (about 1 cup)
1   medium onion, chopped (about ½ cup)
1¾   cups *uncooked* regular long-grain white rice
4   cups Swanson® Chicken Broth (Regular, Natural Goodness® or Certified Organic)
1   teaspoon ground sage
1   can (10¾ ounces) Campbell's® Condensed Cream of Celery Soup (Regular or 98% Fat Free)
¼   cup grated Parmesan cheese

1. Heat the oil in a 4-quart saucepan over medium heat. Add the corn, pepper and onion and cook for 5 minutes or until the vegetables are lightly browned.

2. Add the rice to the saucepan and cook and stir for 30 seconds. Stir in the broth and sage and heat to a boil. Reduce the heat to low. Cover and cook for 20 minutes or until the rice is tender.

3. Stir in the soup. Cook for 2 minutes or until the rice mixture is hot. Sprinkle with the cheese.

KITCHEN TIP

If you want a meatless side dish, substitute Swanson® Vegetable Broth (Regular or Certified Organic) for the Chicken Broth.

Heavenly Sweet Potatoes

Layered Cranberry Walnut Stuffing

Heavenly Sweet Potatoes

MAKES 8 SERVINGS ■ **PREP:** 10 minutes ■ **BAKE:** 20 minutes

Vegetable cooking spray

1 can (40 ounces) cut sweet potatoes in heavy syrup, drained

¼ teaspoon ground cinnamon

⅛ teaspoon ground ginger

¾ cup Swanson® Chicken Broth (Regular, Natural Goodness® *or* Certified Organic)

2 cups miniature marshmallows

1. Heat the oven to 350°F.

2. Spray a 1½-quart casserole with cooking spray.

3. Put the potatoes, cinnamon and ginger in an electric mixer bowl. Beat at medium speed until almost smooth. Add the broth and beat until potatoes are fluffy. Spoon the potato mixture in the prepared dish. Top with the marshmallows.

4. Bake for 20 minutes or until heated through and marshmallows are golden brown.

Layered Cranberry Walnut Stuffing

MAKES 6 SERVINGS ■ **PREP:** 10 minutes ■ **BAKE:** 25 minutes

2 boxes (6 ounces *each*) Pepperidge Farm® Stuffing Mix

1½ cups Swanson® Chicken Broth (Regular, Natural Goodness® *or* Certified Organic)

2 tablespoons butter

1 can (16 ounces) whole cranberry sauce

½ cup walnuts, toasted and chopped

1. Prepare the stuffing using the broth and butter according to the package directions.

2. Spoon **half** of the stuffing into a 2-quart casserole. Spoon **half** of the cranberry sauce over the stuffing. Sprinkle with ¼ **cup** walnuts. Repeat the layers.

3. Bake at 350°F. for 25 minutes or until hot.

▮ KITCHEN TIP

The flavor and crispness of nuts come out when they're toasted, and the nuts are easier to chop when warm. Spread the nuts in a single layer on a baking sheet, then bake them in a preheated 350°F. oven for 10 minutes or until they're golden brown. Stir them occasionally so they toast evenly.

Broth Simmered Rice

Ultra Creamy Mashed Potatoes

Broth Simmered Rice

MAKES 4 SERVINGS ■ **PREP:** 5 minutes ■ **COOK:** 25 minutes

1¾ **cups Swanson® Chicken Broth (Regular, Natural Goodness® *or* Certified Organic)**

¾ **cup *uncooked* regular long-grain white rice**

1. Heat the broth in a 2-quart saucepan over medium-high heat to a boil.

2. Stir in the rice. Reduce the heat to low. Cover and cook for 20 minutes or until the rice is tender.

KITCHEN TIP

This recipe will work with any variety of Swanson® Broth.

Florentine Simmered Rice: Add *1 teaspoon* dried Italian seasoning to broth. Add *1 cup* chopped spinach with rice. Stir in ½ *cup* grated Parmesan cheese before serving. Serve with additional cheese.

Ultra Creamy Mashed Potatoes

MAKES 6 SERVINGS ■ **PREP:** 15 minutes ■ **COOK:** 20 minutes

3½ **cups Swanson® Chicken Broth (Regular, Natural Goodness® *or* Certified Organic)**

5 **large potatoes, cut into 1-inch pieces (about 7½ cups)**

½ **cup light cream**

2 **tablespoons butter**
   Generous dash ground black pepper

1 **can (14½ ounces) Campbell's® Turkey Gravy**

1. Heat the broth and potatoes in a 3-quart saucepan over medium-high heat to a boil.

2. Reduce the heat to medium. Cover and cook for 10 minutes or until the potatoes are tender. Drain, reserving the broth.

3. Mash the potatoes with ¼ **cup** broth, cream, butter and black pepper. Add additional broth, if needed, until desired consistency. Serve with the gravy.

Ultimate Mashed Potatoes: Stir ½ **cup** sour cream, **3** slices bacon, cooked and crumbled (reserve some for garnish), and ¼ **cup** chopped fresh chives into the hot mashed potatoes. Sprinkle with the reserved bacon.